MW01074135

Contiuences ot

Online Marketing

A Holistic Guide

ISBN 978-1-7374091-2-0 (paperback)

Contents

INTRODUCTION.. 1

About this Book.. 3

Tip of an Iceberg 5

PART I: Fundamentals.. 7

CHAPTER 1: The Online Landscape....................... 9

The Avenues to a Website.................................... 11

The Imperative of Strategy.................................... 13

A Confluence of Roles 15

CHAPTER 2: Your Business on the Web............... 19

Business Models Rule 20

Making Definitive Goals...................................... 22

Branding on the Web.. 23

CHAPTER 3: Mapping an Online Strategy 27

Facilitating Objectives.. 27

Knowing Where You Stand.................................... 28

Mapping Routes to Your Website 29

Synergy and Consistency 32

PART II: Websites 35

CHAPTER 4: Websites with Purpose 37

Why Does Your Website Exist? 37

Your Website Objectives 39

Your Website is a Garden 40

CHAPTER 5: Understanding Web Technology 43

Websites, In a Nutshell 43

Performance Matters 45

Hosting – Where your Website Lives 47

Website Platforms and You 50

Open-Source vs. Paid License vs. Subscription ... 55

CHAPTER 6: The Visitor Experience 59

Personas: Knowing Your Visitors, Users, and
Customers 59

Discovering your Personas 61

Personas, Assemble 63

Visitors and Customer Journeys 67

Customer Journeys and Marketing Funnels 70

PART III: Search 73

Chapter 7: How Search Works 75

Search, in a Nutshell 76

Paid vs. Organic Search 77

How Search Engines Know You 79

The Full Picture 82

Chapter 8: Search Engine Optimization, Part 1 85

Chasing Ghosts 86

Content: A King Needs a Court 87

The Wide World of Keywords 89

Keyword Strategy and Tactics 90

Using Keyword Research Tools 92

Keyword Types 94

Building Content around Keywords 98

The Long Game 100

The Specter of PageRank 102

Pagerank and Back Again 104

Content is King, but Backlinks Rule 105

Chapter 9: Search Engine Optimization, Part 2 107

Technical SEO 107

Site Navigation and Structure 108

Your Source Code 111

Metadata 112

Schema Markup 115

Sitemaps 117

Directing Search Engines 119

Mobile-First Search 120

Core Web Vitals: The Need for Speed 122

Local Search 123

Image Search 124

SEO Shenanigans 126

Final Words 129

Chapter 10: Paid Search, Part 1 131

How Paid Search Works 132

Same as it Never Was – The Changing Landscape of PPC 133

The Importance of Landing Pages 135

Knowing Ad Placement Types 136

Keywords, Negative Keywords, and Search Terms 137

Targeting Competitors 139

Paid Search Performance Objectives 141

The Google Ads Hierarchy 146

Chapter 11: Paid Search, Part 2 149

Doing Keywords Right 149

Keyword Matching Types 150

The Anatomy of PPC Ads 153

Creating Effective Ad Copy 153

The Bidding Game 156

Bidding Strategies 157

Your Paid Search Goals 158

PPC Campaigns and Businesses Development .. 159

The Importance of Data 160

PPC Ads and Natural Selection 162

PART IV: The Internet 165

Chapter 12: The Internet at Large 167

Categorizing the Internet 167

The Interplay of Content 170

Maximizing Your Owned Media 172

Owned Media and the External Internet 176

Chapter 13: Paying Your Way 177

The Google Display Network 177

Other Advertising Networks............................. 181

Sponsored Content 183

Affiliate Marketing..................................... 184

Shopping Campaigns.................................... 185

Working With Influencers.............................. 187

Chapter 14: Getting Recognized 193

Trust... 193

The Grey Areas of Earned Media...................... 195

Content is King, Again................................. 196

The Power of Media Kits 198

Getting the Word Out.................................. 199

Targeting Outlets...................................... 201

Finessing Negative Content............................ 202

PART V: Social Media.................................. 207

Chapter 15: Leveraging Social Media.................. 209

Social Media Algorithms............................... 209

Be In the Right Places 211

Meet the Social Media Platforms 212

Chapter 16: Managing Your Social Media Presence
.... 219

Monitor, Listen, and Respond 220

Flaunt Your Authority 222

Network With Others 224

Foster Calls-to-Action 225

The Importance of Consistency.......................... 226

Tread Carefully and Plan Every Message 227

Synergize Content with Social Media 229

Chapter 17: Paid Social Media 231

Social Media Ads vs Search Ads...................... 232

Types of Social Media Ads 233

Meet the Social Platforms, Again...................... 235

Managing Social Ad Platforms 242

The Rising Tide of Data Privacy Concerns........ 244

PART VI: The Online Landscape 247

Chapter 18: Relationship Management 249

Transactional vs Relationship Marketing........... 250

The Importance of Relationships....................... 251

Customer Relationship Concepts 253

Relationships Start with Business Practices 257

Relationships are Built Through Communication
.... 259

Maintaining Engagement.................................. 265

Customer Extension 270

Chapter 19: Putting Everything Together.............. 273

Integrating Online.. 274

Going Offline 275

Revisiting the Online Landscape....................... 278

Measuring Results 281

Key Performance Indicators (KPIs) 282

Traffic Metrics... 283

Beyond Metrics 287

Chapter 20: Staying the Course............................ 289

Never Stop Improving....................................... 290

Survival of the Fittest 291

Staying Future-Proof 292

The Time We Have 298

ABOUT THE AUTHOR.................................... 301

INTRODUCTION

Decades after the dot-com crash and the normalization of internet commerce, much of the cultural conversation continues to marvel over the "newness" of e-commerce. Some of this mentality can simply be attributed to aging Boomers and Gen Xers who remember when the world in which we live today was pure science fiction. Interestingly, we do not consider contemporaneous cultural phenomena like *The Matrix* to be "new" despite its uniqueness and cultural impact. What is it about internet commerce that retains its aura as a new sensation? The answer is two-fold. First, the normalization of internet commerce was revolution in the fabric of our economy and culture. The other reason is that e-commerce and the broader internet continue to be evolving rapidly with no sign of slowing down. This is still happening even after decades of its integration into the cultural zeitgeist. This dynamism is not merely due to technological advancement, but also through expanded expectations in how we interact with the internet and how it should serve us.

The COVID-19 pandemic heralded yet another shift in the ubiquity of internet commerce and its role in daily life. What had previously been conveniences rapidly transformed into necessities. From shopping to food delivery to communication, the pandemic forced us to be more reliant on internet-based services more than ever. Though these changes were not unforeseen, the pandemic accelerated their adoption by many years. Even as the world emerges from COVID-19, the changes in how we all work, shop, and communicate will prove to be permanent aspects of the "new normal".

There is a peculiar thing about internet commerce: Though change is an inseparable aspect of the game, many fundamentals stay the same no matter how disruptive said changes are. Online or not, the psychology behind shopping is the same as it ever was. The wants, needs, motivations of consumers in the bygone days of shopping malls are much the same as they are for someone scrolling on their phone. The internet merely accelerates and amplifies the fundamental psychologies of commerce and communication.

The internet has provided more fertile ground for small businesses than perhaps any time in history. The pool of potential customers is no longer hindered by geographic reach or limited communication. Additionally, businesses need not setup full customer-facing locales to operate – websites are the new showrooms and cash registers.

With such tremendous business opportunities come some significant caveats. The low barriers to entry for online business mean that they face more direct competition than ever before. At every stage of doing business online there are countless competitors clamoring for the attention of potential customers. This need to attract attention is the crux of online marketing. Attention is the principal commodity of the internet. One cannot gain a customer without first grabbing and holding their notice long enough to make your sales pitch. Unfortunately, the internet is an endless cavalcade of attention-grabbing distractions. Not only does a business have to compete with traditional competitors, but also with the cacophony of content on the internet. The mark of an effective online marketer is the ability to grab and hold peoples' attention among all these distractions.

About this Book

The internet is not homogenous and features broad contexture and flavors. This includes online commerce, which does not happen in any singular space on the internet. Typical internet users jump between multiple channels and contexts in their travels. Thus, all avenues for your potential customers must be unbroken, and encompass the milieu of the internet. To do so requires a comprehensive marketing strategy that integrates every channel and context your potential audiences can be found. Online marketing must be holistic - the principal paradigm behind this book

This book provides an overview of the fundamental components of online business and marketing – primarily from a small business perspective. Online marketing is a broad subject with many concomitant sub-topics. You must have a fundamental understanding of them all before you can formulate a truly comprehensive marketing strategy. This book covers each of the major aspects of the internet and how they fit into a synergized marketing strategy. These subjects are discussed in-depth but are by no means comprehensive. This book is intended to be a starting point in your understanding of online marketing, not the end. Regard every chapter as part of a much deeper iceberg, as it were.

This book was written with two audiences in mind. The first are small business owners, leaders, or managers who are either starting out or overhauling their marketing strategy. Such individuals can benefit from this book by getting a sound overview of the landscape of online marketing. The other intended audience are professionals who are specialized in just one aspect of e-commerce. Professionals can skip or skim the parts that cover their field but can gain insight into how their expertise fits into the overall e-commerce picture.

Structurally, this book is divided into six parts. The first is an overview of the fundamentals of online business. Part two discusses how your website fits into the online landscape. The next part is all about search engines, how they work, SEO (search engine optimization), and how their advertising works. Part four explores the internet beyond search and social media. The fifth covers social media in-depth, including managing social platforms, advertising, and working with influencers. The final part of the book puts everything together and how to successfully stay the course.

Tip of an Iceberg

This book is a detailed overview of the world of digital commerce and marketing. However, it is intended to be but a step in a greater journey of learning. After you have finished reading, you will understand the breadth of internet commerce and how its many contexts fit together. Every chapter is a rabbit hole to further research and discovery. It is my hope that you come away from this book with an appreciation of how important interconnection, consistency, and synergy are in online marketing. I extend to you my sincerest thanks for picking up this book and wish you the best of luck in your online marketing journeys!

PART I: Fundamentals

CHAPTER 1: The Online Landscape

The essence of online marketing has always been straightforward: attract an internet users' attention and direct them towards a desired action. This reveals the three-step nature of online marketing: attract, appeal, and action. These "Three As" reduce online marketing to its most basic and reductive conception. It is important to keep this in mind as you proceed deeper into this subject. The abundance of technology and information that comprise the nuance of online marketing can often lead you astray from your principal goals. Evaluating your strategies and tactics in terms of the Three As is an invaluable grounding tool to keep you on track.

Let us now look at these three aspects in a bit of detail, starting with **Attract**. The entire point of online marketing is to utilize the internet to convince someone to perform an action. Of course, before you can even begin convincing them, you need to first grab their attention. This can be a tall order, as the internet is a vast landscape of competing calls to a users' attention. If you are lucky, a user might be on the internet specifically to find your product or service - granting a head-start in marketing efforts. More often, people are on the internet for other reasons or merely distraction, and so you must work harder to pull their attention. Efforts to get a users' attention might not be a first-time success – instead being a matter of consistent exposure and growing familiarity with your business and/or product.

The next step in the online marketing process is **Appeal**. We enter this stage of our relationship with the user only if your efforts to attract them have worked. This crucial stage is often where there is precious little time to convince them that the product or service is worth their continued consideration. This is also a point where many marketers fail by succeeding: they focus exclusively on gaining attention and yet have comparatively little to show users once they have it. A poor showing at the appeal phase means that all the time and expense spent getting their attention went to waste.

The final stage in the online marketing is **Action** - the desired behavior we intend the end user to take. This step is commonly seen as a sales conversion, although it could be any of an array of actions. There are many actions that a potential customer might take that have value to an online business. Sales leads are integral parts of business-to-business (B2B) and/or high-cost product merchandising. Sales leads can range anywhere from emails, phone calls, newsletter signups, or even a social media "like". Many marketers who focus exclusively on sales conversions are missing a huge part of the overall landscape. It often takes time for many people to decide to convert into a sale. However, it takes decidedly less time and risk to offer a sales lead. Additionally, even after a sales conversion, customers retain immense value to marketers afterward in the ever-important practice of relationship marketing. Recent moves by internet companies towards privacy-focused web tracking will make relationship marketing more essential than ever.

The Avenues to a Website

In nearly all cases, your website is the central component of your online marketing world. The importance of having your website function as the central hub of your marketing strategy has to do with control. You have complete control over your site, its content, and the data it generates. Your website is likely the only place on the internet you have direct control, and thus why it is such a critical destination to bring potential customers and leads. Indeed, having a great website is meaningless if you do not understand how to bring in users. Crucially, you need to be bringing in *relevant* users – not necessarily *more*. Quality will always trump quantity when directing website traffic.

More than ever, there are multiple avenues to find a website. As the internet matured, the ways in which people find discover websites has changed and diversified – never again will a single approach to drive traffic like in the old days. It is important to identify and understand the different pathways users can navigate to find your website. Additionally, you must recognize that these routes are simultaneously unique and interconnected in how they drive user traffic to you. In most cases, a successful online marketing strategy will be built around synergizing every avenue toward your website. Short-sighted marketers tend to see each avenue as a separate undertaking of time and expense. However, experts understand that every pathway to a website intersects and compliments each other. To be maximally effective, a online marketing strategy must be holistic and comprehensive.

The avenues of discovering a website can be grouped into three general categories. The first and best known is the search engines. Though the way people utilize search has changed since the early days of e-commerce, their role in research and discovery remain as vital as ever. The next category is social media, which has become a principal way in which people discover new things on the internet – a role once dominated by search. It is here where you have the most direct interaction with end-users than any other part of the internet – perhaps even more than your own website. The third category is the broader internet beyond search and social media. These are websites and destinations where your desired user/customer base frequent. Your access and control of these sites can vary greatly - from paid placements, advertisements, or unsolicited editorial content.

The Imperative of Strategy

Regardless of scale, for an online marketing program to succeed, it must be executed with proper planning and focus. Inexperienced marketers often regard each of their marketing channels as existing in respective vacuums with little regard for how they might complement each other. The promotional campaigns they undertake are often executed with minimal planning and little regard to stylistic or thematic consistency with their branding. They also tend to take short-sighted views of their campaigns by expecting results to be instantaneous with only short-term metrics for success.

The principal difference between a successful digital marketer and an unsuccessful one is strategy. To understand how to think, plan, and operate strategically is to be well on your way to being successful in online marketing or any other endeavor. Strategy is a process. It is the confluence of clear goals, proper research, and prudent planning. These three components should all be present in your approach to your online marketing efforts. First, your goals must be clear – from the specific types of people you are targeting all the way to the precise action you are trying to convince them to take. This ending action, be it a sales lead, email signup, or sale, must be specific and measurable. The second component is proper research. No marketer should press start on a campaign without taking full inventory of the conditions in which they will be operating under. This means taking the time to understand competitors, technology, social trends, business factors, and more. The final component to strategy is planning. This is where your knowledge is directly applied toward achieving your goals. Proper strategic planning is clear, thorough, and organized. Strategically-minded marketers conduct their campaigns methodically and with focus.

The myriad ways you can direct visitors to websites are interconnected. Without persistent tone across all your marketing channels, you diminish synergy among them and sow confusion to prospective customers. Confusion and inconsistency are not feelings you ever want to evoke with your audiences. A strategic approach to your marketing ecosystem is the remedy for this. It forces you to take a holistic view of every avenue in your marketing efforts and ensure they conform to your overall brand identity. Strategy also entails looking at the entirety of your marketing apparatus to see where the various avenues to your website overlap, are complimentary, or lacking. This is a vital concept in ensuring your entire marketing system is as efficient and interconnected as possible.

A Confluence of Roles

Successful online marketing is not an undertaking that involves a single skillset – there are many different "hats" to wear. As discussed earlier in the chapter, there are many avenues a potential customer can take to your website. Every one of these avenues require multiple types of work to be effectively utilized. In addition, your website itself requires multiple skillsets to be technically sound and stylistically compelling. Many business leaders fall into the trap of underestimating the variety of talent that is required to create and maintain a successful online business. Failure to understand these roles and their importance lead to poor leadership and ineffective business performance.

The core of an online business is its website, and it is here where we start looking at the roles required to make it work. Though not every business maintains all these roles in-house, if they have a website, then there is *someone* working in these capacities. Obviously, developers are required to create and maintain websites. What many managers fail to understand here is that web development does not comprise a singular role. The principal division of roles in web development is frontend vs backend. Frontend developers principally work on the appearance and layout of sites. They adapt the designs of the web designer to integrate functionality implemented by the backend developer. A backend developer is a programmer who works on the part of the site that are generally unseen – the database connections, tracking elements, payment modules, shopping cart software, etc. They work on the functional elements that the frontend programmer integrates into the aesthetic design of the site. Backend developers sometimes also act as the website administrator, though this is another role that can exist on its own as well. Web administrators manage the hardware and software that the website itself runs on.

Many people misunderstand what a web designer does, and often incorrectly conflate this role with web development. Web designers determine the look and structure of a site. Web design entails a keen understanding of how people use websites and how to best accommodate them. Web designers are concerned with the usability of a website and how it is to serve the needs of the end-user. Their skills are focused on user experience and aesthetic layouts. Sometimes, frontend developers are also the web designers. However, the expertise required for good web design is different from programming skills, and it is often optimal to have a separate expert in this role.

While programmers, designers, and administrators make sure your website runs properly, they do not fill it with content. This is the job of content creators, graphic designers, and content managers. Graphic designers (along with photographers and other visual creatives) make the graphics and color schemes for the website. They work closely with the web designer to ensure the artistic presentation of the site harmonizes with its usability. They also must communicate with frontend developers to ensure graphics are formatted properly for implementation on the site. Content writers create the written elements of a website- from general informational copy about the company to product descriptions, to customer FAQs. Content writers and graphic designers must be coordinated by somebody acting as a planner- typically a marketing manager. The person filling this role determine what type of content should be on the site. Most often, they coordinate with a larger marketing team. This role is vital in that it ensures a bridge between the website content creators and the overall marketing strategies of the organization.

Marketing roles often include the same talent that manage the content for your website. As will be discussed in detail later in this book, creating content is a principal output of online marketing. This ranges from ad copy, graphics, blogs, social posts, videos, audio, and more. Significant amounts of written and audiovisual content must be generated to feed the myriad marketing avenues required to maintain holistic campaigns. Video and audio content is more normalized than ever before in online marketing – your content output must encompass these formats to stay relevant.

The roles mentioned in this section comprise the most foundational of an online operation. Other roles that play in online business include legal counsel, videographers, and public relations. More recently, companies are having to navigate the ever-increasing public and legislative concerns regarding privacy and personal data. This is to say nothing about other matters of legality and morality such as website usability, privacy, or inclusivity. These matters often require dedicated personnel to ensure they are properly addressed. As the internet evolves, so too will the roles that play parts in making websites happen.

To understand the forest, you must know the trees.

CHAPTER 2: Your Business on the Web

One of the first mistakes many businesses make online is to operate with a poor sense of purpose. Their online mission begins and ends with "we need a website". More than ever, every business should be online to some extent, regardless of their industry. However, the degree to which businesses need to be online varies. This has as much to do with the nature of the business as it has to do with their specific online objectives. The statement "we need a website" is redundant. Canny business owners instead ask: "What are my online goals and what does my online presence need to look like in order to achieve them?"

There is no one-size-fits-all model of what constitutes an optimal online business presence. Nevertheless, it is important to understand the myriad components of online marketing. This is important for two reasons. First, if you want to be a competent digital marketer, you need to keep your knowledge current and comprehensive. Second, the ever-changing nature of the internet means that tech and trends that might be irrelevant to your operation one day might become indispensable down the line. Sometimes, these shifts happen rapidly, and familiarity with the broader internet will make you more able to navigate these shifts when they occur.

The first steps toward creating or overhauling the online component of your business must revolve around two things: your business mode and your online goals. These considerations must be resolved before you begin deciding which aspects of the internet you will utilize. Beware - the temptation to focus on all the cool and interesting tech and trends on the internet can be remarkably high. Make sure that your online strategy leverages the power of the internet to serve your objectives and not waste time and resources on what seems to be "cool" or timely. Heed the cautionary tale of the rush many businesses made to capitalize on buzzy online trends like blockchain and NFTs. Many businesses flocked to these technologies due to their of trendiness without first figuring out if they could actually *help* their business. The result was an immense waste of money and time.

Business Models Rule

The starting point of developing your online objectives revolves around your business model. There are two specific types of models to consider here: the business model and the revenue model. They are closely related but must be independently understood to effectively utilize them. This step is important because every aspect of your online presence must exist in service of either or both. If it does not, then you are wasting time and resources on efforts that create no value.

The textbook definition of a **business model** is how a business creates value for customers. This is what the company does to turn inputs into finished outputs – which can vary from manufactured finished goods to distribution services to support services and everything in-between. It is the processing and delivery of the goods and/or services the business sells. Organizations often have multiple business models. For instance, a software company might design and create software for sale, but also provides support for said software. Though related, both are separate end products.

A **revenue model** denotes how a business generates revenue/income. Revenue models exist as subsets of business models and serve to describe the way goods and services convert into money. Not every business model necessitates the same revenue model and can vary widely depending on the company. For instance, two companies that manufacture roasted coffee beans would have the same business model but could have divergent revenue models: one might sell finished bags of roasted coffee to end-consumers while the other is strictly business-to-business and ships bulk to food distributors. Even similar businesses that sell direct to end-users might have differing revenue models. For instance, one company could be strictly based around one-time-purchases while the other is subscription-based.

Making Definitive Goals

Recognizing the specifics of your business and revenue models is a vital step in developing a marketing strategy. Once you completely understand these aspects of your operation, the next step is to set clear online objectives. You must formulate, in specific terms, what objectives you intend to address via the internet. In most cases, getting the right people to come to your website is a principal objective. The next component is the specific *actions* you intend for these visitors to perform. Most often, businesses are looking for visitors to do one of two things: convert into a sale or generate a sales lead.

Goals are the measurable expressions of objectives. They create the metrics by which your efforts are evaluated for success or failure. These metrics will also provide critical information on next steps in your digital strategy as it evolves. To facilitate this, goals must be specific and quantifiable. For example, say that your online objective is to maximize the sales leads your website generates via an online form. Your next step is to set goals to meet this objective: in this case it might be to "increase sales leads gathered by our website by 20% within three months". This goal is specific in both the desired results and the timeframe involved.

Further refinement of this goal defines a sales lead as an email address provided by a visitor on one or more online forms on the website. Notice how this goal has little room for ambiguity. There is enough specificity where you can measure, after the end of the timeframe, how far ahead or behind the stated goal things turned out. Such information will further help you determine the extent to which your efforts succeeded or failed.

Here, you can see the hierarchy in determining your online goals. Goals are specific expressions of your objectives. Objectives are determined by your revenue model. Your revenue model is a subset of the business model. At the end of this process, you can check your work by asking how your goals ultimately serve your business model and work your way back. This is an essential starting process for effective online marketing.

Branding on the Web

An online marketing strategy is not complete unless it takes your brand into account. Broadly speaking, a **brand** is a feeling. It is the meaning customers attribute to your company and how it makes them feel. Tangible aspects of branding commonly involve graphic design elements like logos, fonts, and color schemes. If your company creates significant content, branding will further include tone, nomenclature, and formality. An especially important contributor to brand perception comes from the quality of your product and requisite customer support.

Part of any business strategy should include how the company and/or product branding should be presented. Do you want to be perceived as trustworthy, professional, large-scale, small-scale, corporate, mom-and-pop, affordable, luxury, etc.? It is important to consciously decide what perceptions your brand should convey. Failure to manage branding can result in confusion and mixed messaging. At best, it is a missed opportunity to maximize the cohesion of your business messaging. At worst, it could inadvertently pick up some negative connotations with customers that might take immense effort to fix.

Determining your brand and its meaning is a fundamental step in establishing how you will go about designing and managing your online presence. It will determine the basis for how your websites, social media, content, and communications will look and feel. Consistent branding will pay dividends in any assorted marketing and promotional efforts you make across the internet. That the many components of online marketing are complementary and overlap in many, and sometimes surprising, ways. Keeping everything on-brand is an effective way at maximizing synergy.

A business without goals is already dead.

CHAPTER 3: Mapping an Online Strategy

Whether you are starting from scratch or overhauling an existing operation, the bedrock of your online marketing efforts must be built upon a concise strategy. It must be complete, coherent, and focused on specific objectives. Creating your strategy will require an investment of time to properly compose. Resist the urge to get started hastily and "figure things out" as you go – a reckless implementation will bring you nothing but wasted resources, missed opportunities, or worse (mistakes can last a long time on the internet). Clearly define your strategy within a document and refer back to it often - especially at times when you feel your online marketing efforts are off-track. Treat your digital strategy document with similar importance and reverence as your organizations' business plan.

Facilitating Objectives

Above all else, your digital strategy must center around meeting your online goals. The first step in this process must be to determine what these objectives are. Review your business and revenue models to answer these questions: Is your website a component of your end product or is it principally for promotion and branding? Do you need just a website, or will you need a social media presence too? Who do you want to visit your sites? What will be the motivation for these visitors to come to your sites? What *specific* action(s) do you want these visitors to ultimately perform on your website? Be sure to use an appropriate level of specificity in determining your strategic objectives.

Knowing Where You Stand

The next step in formulating your strategy is determining the status of your online presence. This is a relevant step even if you are starting out from scratch - some industries and online niches are easier to break into from nothing than others. This underscores an essential component this assessment – knowing the current state of your competitive situation online. This means identifying your principal competitors and determining the extent of their online presence and reputation. You will revisit and build upon this research later when you perform deep-dive competitor analyses. For this specific stage of strategizing, it is sufficient to identify who they are and the degree of their reach.

Aside from competitors, you must determine what the overall state of your industry and market is like online. What are the principal online information sources used by consumers in your industry? Are there particularly popular websites, influencers, and/or forums in this space? Some industries, services, and products types have more online engagement among customers than others. If you operate in a field that has a relatively low amount of online engagement, your competitive advantages and marketing tactics will be different from those with high engagement.

Mapping Routes to Your Website

The next step in assessing your online presence is determining how audiences can navigate to your website. If you are already online, this begins with determining how they can and cannot find you. The next step is figuring what the routes to your website and content should include. Contrast this with your current situation, and you will have an idea on the parts of your online presence you need to focus upon.

There are five principal avenues for potential visitors to find their way to commercial websites: **Search engines**, with both paid and unpaid organic links; **social media**, with paid and unpaid aspects; **external websites** which include news, blogs, forums, and others; **offline promotion**; and **relationship marketing** which utilizes the goodwill and loyalty of existing customers. Remember that these elements interplay closely with one another, and so work within one category will help improve performance in others. This stage of the process is focused on developing a broad view of where you currently stand online. Later, you will be taking deep dives into the details of each aspect in the implementation stages of your strategy.

We start with what you need to know about your search engine presence. Do you currently utilize any paid search advertising services like Google Ads? If so, are you utilizing standard pay-per-click ads or display ads such as the Google Display Network? Aside from paid search, are you getting any significant traffic from non-paid search visits? Do you know what your organic search performance looks like? Are you getting *any* organic traffic from search engines?

Next is social media. Is your business present on any social media platforms, and if so, which ones? As with search platforms, social media offers robust advertising services. Are you currently utilizing any of those? Do you pay anyone on social medial such as an influencer to advocate for your company and/or products? How much engagement do you have with users on social media? Are there any users who advocate for you and/or your product for free, on their own volition?

External websites comprise the broadest online category, and most likely where you will find the most work to be done. Amongst professionals in recent years, this space has been delineated via the **PESO model**: Paid, Earned, Shared, and Owned. These subcategorizations will be discussed in greater detail later in the book. Continuing your online evaluation, ask the following: Aside from search engines and social media, are you paying for advertising placements on any website ad networks? Are there any websites such as news outlets or blogs that promote you without being paid or reimbursed? Do any customers advocate for your company on message boards, blogs or forums? Do you have any bad word-of-mouth shared on any of these places or social media sites? Do you maintain any websites, blogs, or other external pages besides your website and social media?

External websites are also an important aspect of optimizing your own site for search engines. Of the many factors search engines use to determine the relevance of a website are the quantity and quantity of external links. Known as backlinks, these are links from other websites that point to your site. Backlinks and how they work will be covered in detail in PART III of this book.

Though offline marketing has gone out of vogue with the onset of internet commerce, it still has a place. Does your business send any sort of correspondence to potential or actual customers via traditional mail? If so, what type of messages do you send – catalogues, cards, surveys, etc.? If your product is physical, does the packaging provide any information about your websites or social media? Also, for physical products, does the shipping box contain inserts or other promotional materials? Does your business have any way of tracking word-of-mouth referrals?

The final category to audit is your relationship management. This is how you conduct ongoing contact with existing customers. Does your company have any loyalty programs or retention initiatives? Do you have automations or procedures for soliciting repeat business from customers? Do you reward customer referrals? Do you market to existing customers via email or other methods? Does your operation utilize protocols for regular follow-ups with sales leads? What does your customer support service look like? Is it conducive to positive experiences that would lead to repeat business? Does it do the opposite?

Depending on your level of experience in marketing or your time in the internet space, some of the preceding terminology might be unfamiliar. This is perfectly OK, as online marketing is neither rocket science nor alchemy – you should be able to grasp the concepts quickly. Every one of these will be described in detail as this book progresses.

Synergy and Consistency

The secret to effective online marketing comes down to synergy. When properly implemented, every element of your online presence will impact and complement each other. Your social media interactions will help drive mentions of your business elsewhere on the internet which will in turn improve your search engine rankings. Your paid advertising will enforce brand familiarity with potential customers that will make them more likely to convert into paying customers the next time they encounter your business. Everything is interconnected, and so your online strategy must focus on consistency in both tone and design. This is the essence of brand marketing, and why the work you did establishing what your brand identity was such an essential step before building an online strategy. Synergy is key, and your branding is the blueprint to what this should look like.

"Wherever you go, there you are." – Jon Kabat-Zinn

PART II: Websites

CHAPTER 4: Websites with Purpose

Your website should constitute very core of your online presence. It is the one place on the internet where you have complete control over all aspects of the content. In most cases, your website is the principal destination for your prospective customers to find, interact, and ultimately convert into paying customers. It is often the endpoint to marketing funnels and buyer journeys. Your website is where you make both first impressions and final business propositions with potential customers.

The importance of your website cannot be understated, and so its design must be taken with great care. As the backbone of your online operation, it will set the tone for your company branding, mood, design, and marketing. Conceptualizing and designing your site should be one of the most though-out and deliberate steps in the implementation of your online strategy.

Why Does Your Website Exist?

Just as your business should have a mission statement, so too should your website. Why does your website exist? What is its role in the context of your business and revenue models? Where does it fit in regards to your company mission? Asking such questions is essential in determining your websites' mandate. Do not skip this process, as it establishes the basis for all your marketing efforts down the line and the specific goals your campaigns will be planned around.

Where do you begin in this process? Your starting point for establishing the purpose of your site should be your company's' business and revenue models. The revenue model is especially important here because a business website should always facilitate the action steps a potential customer takes on their way to becoming a paying customer. By this point, you should have a good idea what these action steps are. From there, you must determine which of these are going to be served by your website. Before you even begin thinking about site design, you must first know exactly which of these steps the website will facilitate.

The objectives of your website must also consider factors beyond the walls of your business. Customers might have certain expectations from websites operating in your industry. For instance, if most sites in your industry are built around providing press kits and detailed contact forms, you website should be congruent with these expectations. Though there is much to be said about differentiating your site from competitors, it must be done with care. Uniqueness does little for your business if it drastically runs counter to customer expectations.

The other external factor you must consider is your competition. Take the success of your best competitors to heart and understand their strengths. What are they doing right with their website? Which of these strengths can you effectively improve or differentiate upon? Can your website address a customer need that is under-served by the market leaders? Additionally, the paradigms behind the websites of highly successful competitors can reveal much about what works in your industry. These competitors likely spent significant time and money figuring this out as they built their own sites – you can learn from their investments for free. The websites of market leaders reveal what customers expect from websites in your industry.

Your Website Objectives

In all likelihood, your website will need to serve multiple purposes across your business and revenue models. Sometimes, these roles might require very different implementations of website design and tech. In other cases, multiple usages can be addressed together. As you determine your website objectives, you should be grouping them by common implementation. For example, the same form for capturing a sales lead can also be used for gathering feedback. It all comes down to the unique needs of your customers, prospects, and industry expectations.

Consider the following examples of what a declaration of your websites' objectives:

[My] website will...

- ...provide an easy-to-find description of our services.
- ...be the main storefront to find and purchase our product line.
- ...offer samples of our content in exchange for an email address.
- ...facilitate the ability for a prospective buyer to discover our company and request a sales call via a form.
- ...provide an online portal for existing customers to manage their accounts.
- ...be a one-stop location for support articles and manuals for our products.
- ...act as the official outlet for updates on our company, services, and offerings.

Your Website is a Garden

Once you have your objective lists created and organized, you are ready to start the planning and design phase of your site. By grouping similar and related objectives, you have already created a rudimentary outline of the navigation structure of your site. Even in cases where these objectives are dissimilar, the different ways your site will address these should maintain consistent tone, design, and branding. Never design a multi-faceted website in a vacuum – inconsistent design creates customer confusion and diminishes your company branding.

The process of establishing website goals is never a one-and-done affair. Markets and industries change, as do customer needs and business models. In addition, as websites age, they often "drift" in terms of design cohesion, organization, content timeliness, and functionality. As part of your long-term online strategy, you should employ regular re-assessments of your website's purposes and goals. This is best done along with periodic analysis of the state of your industry, revenue model, and competitive situation. Finally, new technology and trends manifest on the internet frequently. To future-proof your business, regular refreshes of your website is essential. In business, stagnation means death, and this rings true more than ever thanks to the internet.

Maintaining a website is not unlike keeping a flower garden. A good garden is meticulously planned in a cohesive manner according to plant coloration, height, landscape, and placement. However, without frequent trimming, weeding, and watering, the garden begins to break down and become unsightly. Every new season introduces the opportunity to add or subtract planting areas or landscape features. As your gardening skills and preferences change, so will the design of your garden. It exists in a perpetual cycle of planning, implementing, maintenance, evaluation, and improvements. A flower garden is never "finished" but is a continual work in progress. If you stop working on your garden, it will fall into disrepair and death. The same is true of a website – it is always a work-in-progress that requires ongoing maintenance and improvements. When you stop maintaining and improving your website, so too shall it wither and die.

"Those are my principles, and if you don't like them...well, I have others." – Groucho Marx

---

CHAPTER 5: Understanding Web Technology

Even if your role is strictly strategic or have no intention of ever writing a line of code, you should know the basics of how websites function. The internet *is* technology and understanding how it works is fundamental to being an effective online marketer. This is doubly important if you are working directly with programmers, SEOs, and designers – you must have a basic understanding of their expertise if you are to collaborate effectively.

Websites, In a Nutshell

The internet is a worldwide network of interconnected computers. The type of computer you are probably most familiar with is referred to as the "client" such as your desktop computer or your smartphone. In accessing a website, your computer is communicating with another type of computer called a "server". The primary role of these machines is to "serve" your client computer whatever content you are requesting access to. Between your client computer and the website server is an array of computers that facilitate this connection.

On your client machine, the user (you) most often uses a web browser such as Chrome or Safari. A browser is a program that facilitates internet access. When you direct your browser toward the content you wish to see, it sends a request over the internet to access it. The browser must first locate where on the internet the content resides, and so asks a type of computer called a DNS Server for directions. DNS stands for "domain name server", which acts as a sort of directory for websites. The DNS server then directs your browser to the main server on which the web content resides.

Once your browser has found the correct web server, it receives a copy of the website in the form of code. The most ubiquitous of this code is the venerable HTML: Hyper-text markup language. This code language describes the layout, appearance, and content of the website, which is then rendered and displayed on the browser for you to view. Along with the code, copies of visual elements such as video, fonts, and graphics are transmitted from the server to your browser. As you navigate through the website, you click links on the page. Each time you follow a link, your browser communicates with the web server for the next web page. In some cases, it sends data from your computer back to the server – particularly if you are transmitting information via forms or other means.

You can probably surmise that the above is a vastly simplified description of how the internet works. There are countless additional steps within the process of requesting and displaying websites. For instance, the transmission of data between your browser and a website often carries significant security risk. An entire subset of web development is centered around ensuring data security and privacy. Bear this in mind when dealing with web developers and administrators – the nuances in their field are vast, and they will appreciate that you understand that.

Performance Matters

When it comes to running a successful business online, never underestimate the importance of website performance. It simply is not enough that your website is serving the correct pages to visitors. Your site must be secure for both your business and your customers. In addition, most internet traffic now comes via mobile devices like smartphones and tablets. Your website must be able to display properly on multiple types of devices. Failure to do so will create a suboptimal experience for your visitors – decreasing the likelihood of them coming back or becoming paying customers. Finally, your website must be fast with pages that load quickly and cleanly. Internet users are increasingly impatient with slow sites and are more likely than ever to abandon a website at the first sign of slowness.

All the above considerations, especially site speed, are primarily (but not completely) determined by the tech your website is built upon. This includes the server it is hosted on, which consists of the physical computer hardware and its operating system. Running on top of these systems is the software application on which your site is built. Your level of control over all this depends on the type of hosting setup you choose and which web applications you are running. Generally, the more direct control you have over your server and software, the more work you need to do to optimize and maintain it. Conversely, utilizing services that maintain these for you is much easier, but can be more costly and might leave you with sub-par optimizations. This is the tradeoff between control and convenience.

Poor site performance is not always due to hosting, server, or software issues. Sometimes, the problem lies with factors which you have limited or no control over. For example, a slow DNS server can affect how your website loads to some users. Another potential problem lies with regional internet accessibility – a particularly challenging problem for local businesses serving customers in an area where internet coverage is lacking.

Hosting – Where your Website Lives

There are several varieties of website hosting to serve sites of virtually every size. To ensure your website is technologically sound, you should start by ensuring it is utilizing the proper type of hosting. Knowing the different breeds of hosting is half the battle – the other half is knowing which is best for your unique website needs. Below are descriptions of the most common categories of hosting.

Dedicated Server Hosting

This type of hosting grants you the most direct control over your website. It is often the costliest option for hosting websites. This is because dedicated hosting grants your site gets a single server computer all its own. No other websites or applications run on this machine – it is 100% dedicated to running your website alone. This means that you have full administrator, or "root", access to the machine. You can configure every aspect of the operating environment in which your site is running. Consequently, you need to have considerable technical knowledge to run such a server – or have someone on your payroll to do so. Dedicated servers are ideal for websites that command large amounts of traffic or have unique technological needs.

Shared Hosting

Shared hosting can be regarded as akin to an apartment building where multiple tenets rent space. Your website is one of several that exist on the same server. This means that you are sharing system resources and bandwidth with other websites. It also means that you have significantly less direct control over your operating environment than a dedicated server. All websites on a shared server must operate under the same software setup and settings. In addition, shared hosting might require you to share IP addresses with other sites. IP addresses are unique identifiers indicating the location of a site or device. This can lead to issues with implementing certain website features, so beware.

Shared hosting is significantly cheaper than dedicated and is ideal for most small and medium-sized websites. It is an ideal first-phase solution for new or smaller sites. If you start with a shared host, you can always upgrade to a more robust hosting setup as you grow. In addition, shared servers are commonly administrated by the company offering the hosting service. Despite having less direct control, this means you do not have to deal as many technical matters as you would with a dedicated server.

VPS – Virtual Private Server

A virtual server is like a hybrid between a dedicated server and a shared one. Technically, the server computer is still physically hosting multiple websites. However, each website is given its own virtual environment – a simulated partition in which to operate much more independently than a purely shared environment.

This setup is less expensive than dedicated hosting and requires less technical knowledge. It still offers significantly more direct control over the technological environment in which your site runs. However, as your site is still sharing system resources with other websites on the machine, it is not ideal for high-traffic sites. Overall, VPS is an effective middle-ground between dedicated and shared hosting. Most small and medium sized sites are well accommodated by this approach.

Cloud Hosting

A relative newcomer to the hosting space, cloud hosting is quite possibly the eventual future of all websites. Rather than living on a single machine, a cloud website is distributed across a networked array of multiple computers. This means that your site exists in a completely de-centralized state. The upshot to this approach is that computing resources like bandwidth are utilized on an as-needed basis. You are not constrained by the limitations of a single machine, virtual or otherwise. This makes your website much more resilient against regional bandwidth constraints – a dedicated host can be affected by localized outages while a cloud distribution is not. Since cloud implementations can vary in terms of configuration and control, they are more akin to VPNs than dedicated solutions.

The biggest advantage of cloud hosting is scalability. Your website will utilize precisely as much computing and bandwidth resources as it needs at a given time. Sudden spikes in traffic that would cripple a single machine are virtually irrelevant with a cloud distribution. The catch here is that your website is treated much like a service or utility – you pay for ongoing service and are charged according to resource usage. In addition, cloud hosting is dominated by a handful of large players in this space – primarily Microsoft's Azure service and Amazons AWS (Amazon Web Services) platforms. Regardless, cloud hosting is ideal for fast-growing operations and sites that are particularly dependent on uptime and performance. Cloud hosting will likely become the dominant way in which websites are served.

Website Platforms and You

Once you have determined which approach to hosting is best for your operation, you must decide what software platform your site will be built on. The days of building websites completely from scratch are long gone, and so your choices will constitute a variety of pre-established services and solutions. As with your hosting choices, the best platform for your website is dependent on your specific online goals and tradeoffs between control vs. convenience.

Your online platform must serve every call-to-action you are seeking from visitors and potential customers. Start your decision process by first making a detailed inventory of what these actions are. For instance, you will likely need to have a way to facilitate an easy way for visitors to contact you. Be sure to differentiate between the different scenarios such contacts will serve – such as support requests, sales inquiries, newsletter signups, or marketing leads. If you are looking to sell goods online through your store, you must be clear on the type(s) of items you are selling: services, media, manufactured goods, digital goods, etc.

Next, you will need to list the "hooks" that your site will have that will entice these visitors to take the actions you listed previously. Will your site serve digital samples? Blog entries? Infographics? Product information? Sales information? Customer support? Creating this list is important not only for designing your website but will also dictate your overall online marketing strategies.

There are many website platforms to choose from. Many of these platforms are capable of multiple types of functionalities, and they continue to integrate more and more features as time goes on. This is a fortunate thing, as you are best served by utilizing as few different platforms as possible – ideally just one if you can. Below is a listing of various types of platforms and features.

Web Content Management Systems – WCMS

Content management system, or **CMS**, is becoming a catch-all term for website platforms – after all, what is a website but a collection of content? Content management systems enable you to create, manage, and curate multiple types of web content. The most straightforward examples of this are blogging platforms such as Wordpress. On the admin backend, you can upload or create online postings and load them onto your website frontend. The software handles much of the formatting and enables you to set the overall look and layout of the site via configuring settings. Years ago, this was done by manually editing the source code of each page. Now, you can do it easily with context menus.

Online Shopping Carts

Shopping cart software are web platforms that facilitate the online sale of goods and services. The basic functions of these solutions include product listings, inventory management, shopping cart functions, payment processing, order management, and user accounts. They are relatively easy to setup – especially with streamlined services like the venerable Shopify. However, these types of shopping carts tend to feature less control and customization as more robust systems. If your online sales offerings and strategies are simple, then you can go with Shopify or its competitors. If your operation is larger or is more complex in its sales paradigms, you would be best exploring the more advanced options, such as Magento.

The type of product you are offering is a major determinant to the type of shopping cart you should use. Simple one-and-done sales can be handled just fine by a simple cart. If you are offering digital goods requiring DRM or other types of authentications, you will need to do your research for the best fit. The same holds true for subscription-based recurring orders or service agreements.

Payment Processing

Accepting payments online is easier than ever but is still more complicated than it might seem to beginners. All-in-one website platforms like Shopify can enable you to accept online payments with just a bank account. More advanced platforms, especially for those that serve larger-scale business volume, will require you setup and configure a merchant processing account and a payment gateway. A **merchant processor** is an entity, usually a bank, that facilitates the actual transfer of funds between a customer and your bank account. **Payment gateways** facilitate the transactions between your website and the payment processor. You cannot have a merchant processor without a payment gateway to connect it to your website.

Accepting payments online involve giving multiple groups a cut of the action. Payment gateways often charge per a few cents per transaction – regardless of whether the payment is accepted or declined. Merchant processors will take a percentage cut of each online sale (some even charge different rates depending on the credit card or other payment type). This is true even for simplified carts like Shopify – they take a percentage and a gateway fee all the same. These rates are semi-negotiable. Processors and gateways will give better rates based on higher monthly or annual sales volumes. Shopify-type services most often have predefined volume tiers for their online payment rates. If you go the route finding your own gateway and processor, you might be able to speak to a representative and negotiate your rates directly – just do not expect any big rate breaks unless you are running large volumes of transactions or revenue.

Open-Source vs. Paid License vs. Subscription

Website platforms are software, and like all software they have different licensing and sales models for their use. The most common variations you will find are open source, paid license, and subscription. Each variety of licensing has advantages and disadvantages including costs and commitments. Some platforms are offered through only one license type while others (such as Adobe's Magento) present multiple options.

Open-Source Licenses

Open-source software is a type of license where the source code is freely available and can be copied and modified by anyone. These applications are usually maintained partly or fully by a dedicated community of end users. Hence, software updates and patches are generally frequent. In addition, the community behind these platforms create a plethora of add-on functionality through modules and other customizations.

One of the most enticing features of open-source software is the pricing – it's free. However, this comes with a major caveat in that you are responsible for upgrades and maintenance of your site. There is no support staff or company standing behind you making sure it is running smoothly. Another caveat is the security of an open-source site. The communities behind these platforms often find security holes quickly and they release patches for them relatively quickly. However, this is a double-edged-sword in that the fact that the source code is available to all, it is easier for hackers to analyze it and find weaknesses to exploit.

Paid Licenses

Paid-licensed software is the more traditional arrangement for software usage. It entails a payment to the original developer for the right to use the software. These are commonly one-time payments for use of the software application, which is then available for you to implement as you see fit. These licenses might include some level of direct developer support. Oftentimes, these developers sell additional service contracts for continued software support and security and/or feature updates. The big advantage of paid licenses over open source is this level of support. You have access to the singular developer of the website platform. They have an economic incentive to ensure it is working properly and securely.

This type of license has its drawbacks, too. In terms of security, the issue here is that detecting and patching security vulnerabilities are the sole responsibility and provenance of the developer. Similarly, this type of software license typically precludes user modification and upgrades. If you want custom upgrades or special features, you are either out of luck or must pay the developer for them to do the work. Finally, this type of licensing generally has the highest up-front costs of the three types – you are paying for a discrete, deliverable product outright. This is before you even consider additional costs like extended support contracts or custom development.

Subscription Model

Finally, there is the subscription model. This is the pricing model for most all-in-one web platforms like Shopify or Squarespace. Many cloud-distributions also use this type of model but tend to have longer-term contract lengths. Here, you pay recurring fee to have your site built and running on the software platform.

The main advantage of this model is the level of support. The product that the service provider is selling is the service itself, and they are heavily incentivized to keep everything running smoothly and securely. This also extends to the usability of the sites on the platform. As a service, site features are concise, functional, and well-documented. Open-source platforms can be scattershot on how well features work – especially if you are implementing features designed by numerous community developers. Licensed platforms are generally one-and-done in terms of feature sets and are not updated as regularly until the next iteration. Cost-wise, subscription licensed platforms tend to be relatively inexpensive compared to paid licenses. This is because the cost is more akin to a rental rather than a full purchase.

Subscription-based platforms are convenient but offer the least amount of control over your website. Unlike the open-source or paid-license models, if you stop paying for the service, your website will go away, and you will likely not have access to its assets or data. It is a lease to exist on the platform for a finite amount of time. While your content, copy, and design elements are owned by you as the copyright holder, the platform on which these exist is not.

"[T]he Internet is not something that you just dump something on. It's not a big truck. It's a series of tubes." – Senator Ted Stevens

---

CHAPTER 6: The Visitor Experience

Good websites are designed around the needs of their intended users. Commercial websites should serve the demands of potential and actual customers. On the marketing side of things, the intent is to convert as many visitors into customers as possible (in a cost-effective manner). This involves both creating content that attracts these visitors and enticements that will move them toward becoming paying customers. Sites that provide ongoing customer support or post-purchase relationships must deliver on these to effectuate customer retention and positive word-of-mouth. Sites that fail to effectively deliver on these needs can cost a business dearly - from low sales conversions to poor customer retention.

Personas: Knowing Your Visitors, Users, and Customers

Before you can design your website and its attendant content, you must know who you are trying to accommodate. This introduces the concept of personas - an invaluable and time-tested marketing design methodology. A **persona** is a hypothetical person who represents a key segment of your target audience. Depending on the type of product or service you are offering, your business likely has several types of "typical" customers. This even holds true for commodified or ubiquitous products. For instance, everyone buys shoes but personal interest, income, and style preferences drive different people to different places to buy them. Additionally, most businesses will have multiple personas that make up their customer base. Depending on your business and industry, you might find that you have dozens of personas that comprise (or should comprise) your customer base.

Personas do not have to include only your ideal customers either – it helps to create personas for unlikely or undesirable types of customers. Part of attracting potential customers is filtering out those who are decidedly *not* a potential (or good) customer. These "negative" personas are invaluable in creating content and strategies to filter them out. If you have been in business long enough, you surely have encountered varieties of customers who end up costing more money to accommodate than the revenue they generate. Avoiding these types of personas help minimize unprofitable customers. It also helps save you money by not wasting your marketing budget on targets that don't convert into customers.

A persona must fulfil two requirements. First, it must be broad enough to represent a typical example of a key portion of your target customer base. A "key" portion need not always be a large quantity of your base – customers who spend larger amounts of money or are more likely to convert into a sale can be key to your business even if they are relatively few. Second, your personas must be specific enough to differentiate crucial characteristics about them. For instance, you might have two sets of shoe customers who are similar in every major way, except that one is a shoe collector, and the other is not. Maximizing sales here requires special accommodation be made for each of these types.

Discovering your Personas

The challenge in developing personas is selecting the correct demographic and psychographic factors that best describe the "average" representative of each key audience segment. Effective personas are not developed via guesswork – they take extensive research and insight to discover. They are comprised of two general components: their demographics and their psychographics. Broadly speaking, **demographics** denote *what* a persona is, and **psychographics** represent *who* they are. Demographic factors include age, gender expression, sex, occupation, ethnicity, income level, and geographic location. Psychographics include lifestyle, hobbies, interests, political leanings, entertainment preferences, and adventurousness.

The first place to start in the persona development process is to learn about your existing audience. If you are already an established business, you likely have an extensive list of paying and potential customers. Depending on the granularity of this data, you might already have significant demographic information to go on. If not, your task lies in procuring information about your industry and your niche in it and extrapolate the demographic and psychographic profiles from there. Many industry trade groups maintain such databases and there are many research firms that maintain similar data sets.

Make use of every resource you have in learning about your customer base. Customer service and sales personnel have direct interactions with your customers, and so have valuable insight about them. Query these individuals about what they learned about your customers via these relationships. You might also want to set a protocol for your customer-facing staff to ask customers certain (optional) questions about themselves. Do not rely 100% on subjective assessments by you or your colleagues regarding your customer base. They are valuable anecdotes but represent only one source of demographic and psychographic information.

Perhaps the most effective way to learn about your customer base is to ask them about themselves directly. This is done by the time-honored practice of customer surveys. This can be effectuated in multiple ways, such as direct mailings, emails, or even (brief) point-of-sale online surveys. If you choose to do a survey among your existing customer base, you need to be aware of a few things. First, DO NOT SPAM. Spamming unsolicited survey requests are not only off-putting to many people, but it can run you afoul of email ISPs or worse. Next, your sample size should be large enough to infer real knowledge from the survey – if you sample too few customers, you will not have a realistic picture of the overall group. Finally, you should incentivize responses. You are asking for a favor from your customers in the form of their time and personal data. Offering a coupon, discount, or other perk that is a fair trade will generate more replies.

Your business industry and market niche are huge indicators of the types of customers you have – or *should* have. In this age of big data, there is an immense amount of market data available for virtually every industry and niche. This market research data is not always free, and the paid sources will always be better and more comprehensive. Data from reputable market research firms is comprehensive and is often well-worth the cost if you can afford it. I recommend you always budget for purchasing market research when doing a demographic analysis. The saved research time alone justifies much of the cost.

Personas, Assemble

Once you have completed your customer research, you are ready to build out your personas. Recall that these are hypothetical individuals that represent a typical representative of key parts of your customer population. These fictional characters should be described specifically enough to drive home what defines their niche in your customer base. The aspects of their hypothetical lives you will be defining should include their basic demographics, lifestyle, values, professional background, and their shopping motivations - AKA "pain points". What are **pain points**? People tend to shop for goods or services to solve a problem. These problems are caused by these circumstantial pain points.

In online marketing, an essential part of the customer persona is their level of online presence and engagement. While most people tend to be online in some capacity, the amount and depth of their presence can vastly vary. Your websites need to be able to cater to the internet habits of your core personas if you wish to maximize your success. This includes not only to the structure of your website but also in how you drive them to your site in the first place. After all, you do not want to waste money advertising on Facebook if your key personas are younger and less likely to be there.

To give you an idea of how a persona should be compiled, look at the following examples. Note that they are given "real" names. This helps to further humanize their conception. The practice also makes it easier for marketing teams to be on the same page when utilizing personas in their work.

"Bob"

- Male; Age 31; Atlantic City, NJ
- Occupation: HVAC technician; $65k
- Lifestyle: Married, no children. Likes to watch F1 races. Fishes on the weekend. Does not travel often.
- Personality: Introvert.
- Shopping Behavior: Prefers to shop online. Relies heavily on product reviews and Influencers. Does not buy readily and needs several days to make a purchase decision. Loyal to stores and brands he likes.
- Internet Presence: Not interested in social networks. Enjoys watching YouTube content.
- Motivations and pain points: His work is interfering in his leisure time. Wants to streamline his fishing equipment so he can maximize time at the lake and less time packing.

"Nancy"

- Female; Age 26; Dallas, TX
- Occupation: Environmental Science; $60k

- Lifestyle: Single. Frequent traveler. Avid reader of assorted non-fiction. Plays videogames.
- Personality: Outgoing.
- Shopping Behavior: Impulse shopper. Frequently leaves user reviews. Price conscious.
- Internet Presence: Avid Instagram user. Plays online videogames. Does not own a desktop computer – smartphone dependent.
- Motivations and pain points: In the market for a desktop computer.

"Mary"

- Female; Age 43; Albany, NY
- Occupation: Graphic Design; $40k
- Lifestyle: Divorced. Enjoys cooking. Owns two parrots. Hikes every weekend. Camps every other month.
- Personality: Introvert. Reserved.
- Shopping Behavior: Prefers to shop in-person. Does product research online. Dependent on product reviews. Prefers to buy from socially responsible businesses.

- Internet Presence: Limited. No social media accounts. Browses twitter for product and company research.

- Motivations and pain points: Recently divorced and in need of house supplies and furniture. Adapting to newly reduced household income.

The above examples show just one approach to how a persona can be depicted. Some marketers draft their personas to resemble online dating profiles as they might be written by the personas themselves. Other approaches depict personas in the fashion of a job application and resume. I once worked with a marketer who depicted their personas using a Dungeons and Dragons character sheet!

Visitors and Customer Journeys

Every visitor who interacts with your website, or even just your broader online presence, is somewhere on a pathway in their relationship with your company. Oftentimes, these visitors interact a few times or even just once with your business and then they move on forever. Every one of your customers be they prospective, active, or former, exist on some stage of a continuum called the **customer journey**.

From a marketing and web design perspective, your challenge is to facilitate this journey and lead your potential customers on the path toward becoming paid customers. Understand that this is not an endpoint, but rather a new beginning. Some products and services require an ongoing relationship and online accommodation as part of delivering those products. You will need to continue to nurture existing customers into repeat customers again and again – it costs far less time and money to retain repeat business than to acquire it anew.

Your online strategy must be built to facilitate all these journeys, and that begins with your personas. Each persona has a unique journey on their way to becoming a paid customer and beyond. Your websites and extended web presence must be setup to interact with these personas along the way on their journeys. These interactions are often referred to as **touchpoints** and include anything as mundane as merely seeing one of your online ads all the way to direct communication or payment with the company.

All customer journeys fall upon the same general stages:

Awareness

The first stage is **Awareness**, which is the point at which a potential customer realizes they have a problem or desire or need to mitigate.

Research

Next comes the **Research** phase of the journey. This is where the prospect is actively searching for a solution to the need they were previously made aware of. This is the stage at which you will have your fist touchpoint with them. Depending on the nature of the customer and the product/service you are selling, there might be several touchpoints in this phase.

Decision

Next, the customer enters the **Decision** phase in which a purchase is imminent. At this point, they have narrowed down their options on what they will buy and from whom. Any touchpoint at this stage is extremely critical to success in getting the sale.

Purchase

Finally, there is the **Purchase**. This is nearly always the point where money is exchanged, and someone (hopefully you) has beat out the competitors and won the sale. However, the sale is only complete when it is successful - if your website is technologically unsound or has a poor checkout process, you can see the sale slip through your fingers. Customers have very little tolerance for difficulty in making online transactions.

Post-Purchase

The **post-purchase** phase of the journey is dependent on the nature of the product or service. Small, inexpensive, and one-off products are less likely to create a long-term customer relationship. Expensive purchases often involve a longer buyer journey with more touchpoints, and so makes it easier to facilitate a customer relationship. In any case, offering ongoing support and follow-up correspondence goes a long way toward generating trust, word-of-mouth, and repeat business. Your online branding and social outreach are also a big part of your post-purchase strategy. Customers were already convinced to do business with you, and so are worth maintaining their mindshare on social channels.

Customer Journeys and Marketing Funnels

You might have encountered a concept called **marketing funnels** (sometimes referred to sales funnels, or even just funnels) that appear to have a lot in common with customer journeys. In fact, they both tell the same overall story of a visitor moving from a prospective to paying customer. They principally differ in strategic and tactical purpose. The customer journey defines the stages they take on their way to converting into a sale and beyond. It lays out the naming convention of the various steps on the path.

Marketing funnels are primarily focused on revenue – the endpoint is typically the action step, which is usually the point-of-sale. The term "funnel" derives from a visualization of the journey. The top level of the funnel is the first stage of the journey and constitutes the largest pool of individuals. As you move down the funnel to subsequent stages in the journey, the width gets progressively narrower – fewer and fewer prospects make it to these next levels as their interest wanes, find alternatives, or cycle out of the process.

Marketing funnels define and visualize specific plans and strategies to move customers through their journeys. Hence, funnels are more specific than journeys, and are used to delineate specific marketing plans, promotions, websites, and campaigns that work at each stage on the path. Where the customer journey is a single generalized set of steps, there can be multiple funnels along the way. You might have a marketing funnel for each one of your personas, or for different marketing paradigms. For instance, you have a funnel that is designed to cater to personas who are heavily engaged on social media, another for personas who rely on video reviews, and yet another for customers who are seldom online.

Finally, while customers all have the same journey from prospect to paying, they might get there via multiple funnels. One mistake some marketers make is that they presume a persona will convert into a customer via a single funnel catered to them. However, human behavior can be quite complex. You may well have a customer who first becomes aware of your company through a social media-focused funnel but end up jumping to your influencer-oriented funnel and converting the rest of the way there. Everything is interconnected, and so too must your marketing plans. In this regard, you should think of your funnels as parallel to one another – all serving the same overall buyer journey. Plan to have at least one (more is ideal) funnel for every type of persona you identify, but always ensure that they allow for users to jump between different marketing paradigms. The more you isolate your funnels, the less flexibility you have in accommodating the full breadth and potential of your prospective customer base.

Before you cook someone dinner, know what they like to eat.

PART III: Search

Chapter 7: How Search Works

You will be hard-pressed to find an internet user who does not utilize search engines. Regardless of industry or niche, accommodating search engines is the most pervasive component of promoting a website. Experts once claimed that the explosive growth of social media would be the end of search as a principal avenue to finding websites and brands. This turned out not to be the case as search engines continued to adapt to every major online paradigm shift. Search remains important and is not going away.

We principally use search engines for research, entertainment, or shopping – none of which are mutually exclusive. The principal reason people use online search is for research. This research may be in service of merely locating information, entertainment or finding products to buy. Additionally, initial search intent does not necessarily determine their ultimate destination or outcome. For instance, someone looking for information on how to fix a loose doorknob ends up buying a specialty screwdriver during their research. Another example is someone looking to buy a new Marvel action figure and ends up watching a YouTube video about the current state of Marvel Comics. The takeaway is that while search users might begin with specific intentions for research, shopping, or entertainment – the interconnectivity of information can lead to multiple outcomes.

Search, in a Nutshell

Search engines are services that explore the vast amount of information and content on the internet. These engines, using programs known as "**crawlers**", "**bots**", or "**spiders**", catalogue this information in databases known as "**indexes**". Search engines never stop exploring and cataloguing the internet, and websites are frequently revisited to keep the indexes current.

When you input a word or phrase into a search engine, the software compares your request to their indexes. Using extensive algorithms and artificial intelligence, the search engine returns to you a list of websites that best match what it thinks you are looking for. Most search engines will also return results from websites who pay for the privilege of being listed there. These paid listings are also subject to algorithms to ensure that they are relevant to what you are looking for. However, these listings also give priority to whoever is willing to pay the highest for your click – there will be much more about this in chapters 10 and 11.

Search on the internet is a constantly changing and inconsistent affair. New websites are always coming online, and most extant sites routinely update and expand their content. In addition, search engines are in an unending war of attrition with search marketers. Search marketers employ an approach called **Search Engine Optimization or SEO** in their efforts to get their sites to appear higher in organic search listings. **Organic search** results are highly desirable in search because they bring in higher amounts of website traffic without the costs associated with paid search results. Search marketers are constantly trying to figure out how to trick or game the search engine algorithms. Conversely, search engines are endlessly adapting to these tactics. A search engine that can be manipulated will provide suboptimal results for users. Search engines depend on user trust to survive – nobody wants to use one that does not return relevant results.

Paid vs. Organic Search

There are two distinct sides to online search: organic and paid. Though they are very different beasts in terms of how they end up on results pages, they appear in the same place for all search users. To many (perhaps most) end users, the difference is negligible so long as they are being shown results that are relevant to what they are looking for. For online marketers, the differences are huge and require distinct approaches in how they accommodate them. Both paid and organic search results involve catering to search algorithms and best practices. Search engines have an incentive to ensure their end users are getting relevant results to their queries, paid or not.

Websites that appear on organic search results get there because the search engine algorithm has determined that they are relevant to the user's search query. Organic results are displayed in order of relevance – the more relevant the algorithm believes the site to be, the higher up on the list it appears. These search results lists are known as **Search Engine Results Pages**, or **SERP**s. Search marketers track and use this positioning as the principal indicator of a web pages' optimization for the search term in question.

Contrasting starkly with organic results, paid search results appear based on how much the site advertiser is willing to pay, along with how relevant their listing is to the search terms. The websites to which these advertisements link do not factor in whether they appear on a search results page or not. However, as these placements are paid, the advertiser has an incentive to have something relevant to the search results unless their goal is to throw away money. Nevertheless, search engines require advertisers to adhere to best practices to ensure their ads are relevant. Just as with organic search, they rely on users trusting the relevance of their results. Like organic results, search advertisements are listed in a specific order – more relevant and/or higher budget ads generally appear higher on the list.

A reductive way to think of organic vs paid search results has to do with who is competing for placement. Every relevant website (that are in the search engine indexes, at least) is competing with one another to appear in organic results – the more relevant to a given search query, the better their chances to appear near the top of the results list. Paid search is a competition not between websites, but advertisements and their respective marketing budgets. The more relevant the advertisement is to the search term and how much the marketer is willing to pay will determine if the ad is shown on a results page.

How Search Engines Know You

Search engines are powered by vast repositories of information cataloging the content of the internet. Google, the largest search provider in the world, indicates that their index covers *trillions* of web pages. How does a search engine even collect this information in the first place? To understand this, you need to understand how search engine crawlers work. Recall that crawlers (AKA spiders, or bots) are programs that scour the internet and identify the content of every web page they encounter. These programs are designed to visit, or crawl, websites and follow links to and from them. As the crawler reads the source code of each web page, it looks at the various elements of the page to figure out what it is about. The crawler will follow links within the web pages to get a feel for the structure of the website and the content of its other pages. Links that lead to and from the page also provide clues as to what the page is about.

Finding New Sites

Search engines must be able to find a website in the first place. Back in the day, they were more reliant on human actions like website submissions or listings on curated web directories. Today, crawlers are sophisticated enough to locate most new websites and content without human intervention. Crawlers don't visit sites one-by-one, but instead they "surf" the internet, following outbound links from one site to the next. Search Engines pay attention to where these links are coming from and going to – having many incoming links to a site is often a strong indicator of subject relevance or popularity. Search engines have also adapted to the new age of social media by crawling those sites and using them to find and catalogue and index content shared by users.

You can still manually submit a website to search engines, which can help new sites get noticed sooner. This can be done very easily through the respective free toolsets search engines provide. For instance, Googles' Search Console allows you to submit the URL for your new site as well as sitemaps (covered in Chapter 9). Beware of the many grifters on the internet who offer to submit your sites to search engines for a fee – these services are always rip-offs.

Reading Your Code

Search crawlers read websites at the source code level, and so "see" web pages in a different way. If your website is properly optimized for search engines, a web crawler can glean more about the content of your site than even your human visitors. In the past, search marketers were able to manipulate search engines through the shady use of coding tricks. These days, search engines are not so easily fooled. In fact, harsh ranking penalties await websites that attempt to untowardly manipulate them.

One of the first things search engines see in your website source code are various headers and metadata. **Headers** are identifiers in your code that identify the various types of content on your site. Headers indicate where your site titles are, as well as the various blocks of content within. Similar to headers is metadata. **Metadata** describes the content within elements of your site. It often works with headers to give crawlers an idea of the structure of your site: Headers indicate the *type* of information while metadata describes *what* that information is. Another invaluable use of metadata for search engines are those for images, video, and other such multimedia content. Search engines are still not great at determining the content of multimedia, and so rely on metadata to understand what this content contains.

As an aside, metadata can also help with the usability of your website. Hearing and sight-impaired web users utilize software that parses websites in a way they can better understand. Like web crawlers, these programs read the source code of websites to determine a complete picture of the content within. Good headers and metadata are the first (not last) step in creating fully accessible websites.

The Full Picture

The code, structure, and content of a website are only part of the search equation. Search engines care about technical aspects of websites more than ever, and their crawlers take note of this. Site speed, organization, and how it displays on mobile devices are factors that influence organic search rankings. This is to say nothing about how good the actual information on your website is for users. Online search is perpetually evolving, and changes as both the nature of the internet changes and the "tricks" search marketers employ to manipulate it. This is why staying current on search and internet trends is essential for online strategy.

Search determines whether an online businesses lives or dies.

Chapter 8: Search Engine Optimization, Part 1

If you want your website to reach an audience, you must cater to the search engines. You can surely pay for traffic via search ads and other placements, but unless it is consistently converting into steady revenue, such an approach is unsustainable. Your site needs to be bringing in a significant amount of "free" traffic to be viable in the long-term. This begins by ensuring your website is optimized for search. Welcome to the world of search engine optimization, or SEO.

One of the upshots of SEO is that much of its implementation improves the quality and marketability of websites beyond search. SEO helps sites be all they can be by addressing both technical performance and quality of the content. Because search engines are focused on topical relevance and usability, good SEO makes for better websites.

At its core, SEO is a series of best practices intended to maximize both the searchability of a website and the quality of its content. Search engines cannot properly index a webpage that isn't configured to be crawled by them. Even web pages with great content will be short-changing themselves by failing to be fully readable to a crawler. Increasingly, search engines are evaluating the usability of websites. Websites that are slow, clunky, or display poorly on mobile devices are being penalized in their search rankings. Where SEO was once focused only on website content and structure, it has evolved into a holistic practice including performance, cohesiveness, organization, and usability.

Chasing Ghosts

The practice of SEO ultimately revolves around catering to search algorithms – particularly Google, the dominant search provider. These algorithms are always evolving, improving, and retooling as the internet evolves. Changes in search algorithms can create sudden shifts in how websites rank on organic search results. In most cases, search engine updates achieve their intended goal – to make search results more relevant, reliable, and less prone to manipulation by unscrupulous search marketers. Just as these algorithms change, so do the best practices for optimizing websites for search.

The SEO industry is often mired in a perpetual game of guesswork and extrapolation on how search algorithms work and the effect updates have on rankings. Search companies obviously do not divulge much on how they function or what adjustments them make. This is important to ensuring search results are immune to manipulation. Regardless, many SEOs spend much of their working hours trying to divine how search engines work and how to manipulate them. Thus, we see a typical cycle in SEO: Google makes a change; someone thinks they figured out what happened; SEOs flock to adjust their search tactics to compensate; repeat. While staying abreast of current trends and changes in search is essential to search optimization, it often becomes the singular focus of many SEOs. The entire point of algorithm updates is to move closer to this objective – provide the most relevant results for a given search. Obsessing over the latest cryptic message or update from Google distracts from this central tenet of search. As search engines strive to provide topical relevance for search users, so too is this the focus of good SEO with search algorithms.

Content: A King Needs a Court

One of the tritest terms in SEO and online marketing is "Content is King". Make no mistake: content is the reason why people visit websites in the first place. Search engines will always be primarily focused on scanning the content of a website. Sites with poor or irrelevant content seldom make it to the top of search results regardless of how technically sound they are. The few sites that do (usually by shady means) always fall off search quickly, and quickly leave when they realize how poor the content is. If you want to succeed online, you must have compelling content. Period.

Website content can include just about anything. At its most basic and numerous are text, blogs, and articles. Content can also consist of multimedia including infographics, video, community discussions, podcasts, and streams. Different types of content serve different usage scenarios. For instance, watching a video requires a bigger time commitment from users than reading an article – it is easier to gleam information by skimming text than scrubbing through a video. Short-form content serves different usage needs than long-form content. The balance of the types of content your website should have is dependent on your target personas. Remember, your site is still principally designed around catering to your target audiences and their interests.

Unfortunately, having great content is not a panacea when it comes to getting your website found on the internet – let alone search. It simply is not enough to create the content and expect visitors to show up on their own. If you only build it, they will not come. Your content must have attendant optimizations for it to drive search traffic to your site. In addition, your content must be structured in a way to let the search engines know what it is about and who your best audience is. Finally, search engines place heavy emphasis on whether other websites are linking to your pages. This might not seem fair, especially if your content is great, but you are playing the search engines' game – not yours.

The Wide World of Keywords

Search engines base their indexes around **keywords**. Keywords are words or short phrases that indicate the subject of the pages on which they reside. Generally, the more frequent keywords and their close approximations appear on a page, the more likely the page is about that subject. Search algorithms are sophisticated enough to understand associations between different keywords that frequently pair around certain subjects. They are also intelligent and getting "smarter" all the time. They can determine if a webpage is providing useful content or is arbitrarily filling itself with redundant keywords in a futile attempt to game the system.

Keywords are often conflated with **search queries**, or **search terms**. Though related, there is an important difference between them. Search queries are the myriad phrases users enter into search engines. Keywords are the "key" words and phrases that are common to longer search queries in a given subject. For instance, see the following examples of search queries for users looking for information on how to repair drywall:

- **drywall repair**
- **repair drywall**
- **repair drywall** myself
- how to **repair drywall**

- damaged **drywall repair**
- help **repair**ing **drywall**
- DIY **drywall repair**s
- **drywall repair** guide
- can I **repair** damaged **drywall** myself
- help with **drywall** and doorway **repair**

Notice the bolded words in the above examples. These are the keywords. Regardless of how long or short the search terms are, the keyword phrase isolates the essence of what the users are searching for. Keywords are important for maintaining search indexes because it is nigh impossible to index every possible search term for a subject. These constitute the "key" in keywords.

Because keywords are so important to search engines, they are of great importance to search marketers. Just as with the search indexes, you do not have to build your pages around every variation of your desired audiences' search terms – you need to direct your focus on the keywords.

Keyword Strategy and Tactics

If you want your website to reach the right audiences, you need to have a keyword strategy. You must first know which keywords you should be targeting. Next, you will need to craft your site content around accommodating these keywords. Finally, your keyword strategy will shift to a continuous cycle of performance evaluation and revisions. Keyword strategy is about focus, consistency, and perpetual improvement. Markets, customers, and search engine algorithms all change – and so must your strategy.

In making your keyword lists, it is advisable to start out in an organized fashion. You will need to sort, filter, and expand this list in the future. The best way to do this is with spreadsheets. As you brainstorm, discover, and research your keywords, be sure to include references for each entry as to where in this process you entered them. Your personas will factor into this process too – you want to attribute your keywords to them as well.

The first step in your keyword strategy is building your keyword list. This list will dictate your website content. Building this list is a process known as **keyword research**, or **keyword planning**. The importance of your primary keyboard list cannot be understated, and you should plan to spend a significant amount of time working on it. Depending on the size and scope of your online goals, it could take several days to compile. Do not take shortcuts here.

Your keyword list starts with brainstorming. Start with the obvious keywords that are applicable to your brand, product, and industry. Next, determine the stand-out keywords surrounding your website goals and objectives. If one of your site objectives is to get visitors to sign up for an informational newsletter, what kind of web searches should lead them to your website? This stage of brainstorming is where you bring out your list of personas and determine the kind of searches they might be conducting to find you. Remember to attribute your personas to these keywords in your list.

Using Keyword Research Tools

Brainstorming and conjecturing keywords can only get you so far - you will eventually need to employ hands-on research. If you have close competitors, the keywords they target can provide valuable insight into where your targets should be. You can gleam insight into these keywords by looking at competitor's website source code. Every major web browser has options that let you do this. However, considering that most sites contain multiple pages, this part of this process that is best served by a tool.

There are many great tools and services that aid in all aspects of keyword research. These tools work best if you already have a sizeable set of keywords to start with. If you completed your brainstorming work, then you are ready to go here. There are both "first party" and "third party" options in this space. Google and Bing both provide free keyword tools. Google is so dominant in search that you are best using their **Google Keyword Planner** for all your research. Though Google offers this tool to encourage use of their paid search offerings, it does just fine for researching organic keywords. There are several excellent third-party keyword planning tools available, including the venerable SEMRush, Moz, and Ahrefs. These tools offer more extensive feature sets that aid in all aspects of web management, but they can be expensive.

Though they differ in some feature sets, keyword tools offer generally similar functionality. For keywords, these tools provide suggestions for additional terms beyond your initial list. They will generate lists of similar and synonymous terms as well as variations. You can set how broad or specific you want suggested keywords to be – it is important to have variations of your terms with different levels of specificity. You can also input sample search terms your prospective visitors might use, and the tool will generate suggested keywords around those. These tools also let you run analyses of competitor websites and generate lists of keywords their sites are optimized for.

Keyword planning tools also provide valuable information on the popularity of keywords. This is an essential piece if intelligence for keyword strategy. Highly competitive keywords are those where many websites are competing on search engines to display on results pages. Keywords that are competitive tend to be that way because they are broad. The broadness of these terms means that the web traffic they generate can be quite large. More traffic equals higher competition in getting ranked for them. Less competitive keywords are easier to rank in search results but have comparatively lower traffic. Pursuing generic, broad, or otherwise high competition keywords is most often an imprudent strategy. You need to spend your resources on optimizing for keywords that you can realistically rank for. Additionally, high-traffic keywords tend to be quite broad, meaning that much of any traffic coming in will be "bad" visitors who are not necessarily interested in the specifics of your website.

Keyword Types

Not all keywords are created equal, nor do they all serve the same purpose. To better understand how search keywords work, it is important to know the differences and why they are important. Deeper and more advanced SEO necessitates ever increasing granularity in how keywords are categorized. Below are the most common types you will encounter in general SEO.

Seed Keywords

Seed keywords are sometimes referred to as **short-tail** keywords. They are generally very short and rarely more than one or two words. These keywords are also broader in terms of subject matter and thus tend toward higher search volume and competition.

An example seed keyword would be *home repair*. This term is obviously searched very often and is thus very hard to rank for. However, as home repair is a vast subject, much of this search volume is mixed with people looking for a huge array of information. You don't want to use this keyword as one of your targets, but it sets the groundwork for generating better keywords that narrow down this broad audience. Hence why it is called a "seed" keyword.

Long-Tail Keywords

Long-tail keywords are so named by the how they appear on a graph analysis of variant search terms. If you analyze monthly online search traffic for *home repair* along with variations and expansions on the term – you will notice that there is a long list of lower-traffic keyword variants. These additional keyword phrases do not have nearly as much traffic as their seed keyword, but taken as a whole, they generate as much or more. Examples might include *home drywall repair, housing fix-its*, or *local help for home repair.*

Targeting these keywords and key phrases instead of the broader term is a wise investment of time and effort. For one thing, they are lower competition and thus easier to rank for. Second, they are more specific terms and thus more likely to bring in visitors who will convert into buyers. Finally, if you successfully target enough of these long-tail keywords, you can generate the same type of traffic numbers you would get from a broader high-competition keyword.

Brand Keywords

These are types of keywords that cover your business and/or product branding. These terms always include your brand terms, company names, and slogans. Brand keyword content is typically spread across websites across most or all their pages – in addition to dedicated "about" pages.

Competition Keywords

It might seem sneaky or unethical to directly target your competition with your keywords. Admittedly, this is a murky topic, and all depends on how you approach it. Competition keywords are terms that are directly reflect the branding and names of your competitors. On one hand, this makes perfect sense as your potential customers are as likely to be looking at competing brands as yours. However, targeting competitor brands by name means usage of their names and terms – many of which might be trademarked.

Tread carefully if you If you do go this route. Targeting these keywords means using them as part of your site content. Your usage must be sparing and factual – the most direct you should get is with product/service comparisons. Businesses often monitor where their brands and trademarked terms show up online and targeting these will eventually put them on their radar screen. Do not be surprised if you get an email for a saber-rattling lawyer or two.

Variant Keywords

While you cannot effectively predict search terms, you can predict variations on keywords. Variant keywords comprise permutations on your existing keyword list. Common variants include plural versions, common misspellings, hyphenated words, hyphenated phrases, and close synonyms. Do not ignore variant keywords. Some keyword research tools will generate these for you. If not, you would do well to take the time to do it manually.

Oftentimes, these variant keywords are uncommon, low-competition terms. As with long-tail keywords, targeting these variants is an effective way to gain organic search traffic that can become substantial in aggregate.

Keyword Families

Closely linked keywords, particularly variation terms, are best utilized in groups. These groupings most often include variations and synonyms of a seed keyword. In addition, some key terms are so often combined with one another, that most content that covers one keyword also covers the other one. In creating these keyword families, you will gain a clear picture on which words can be covered with the same content pages on your website. This saves work and helps focus your site content.

Building Content around Keywords

Once you have compiled your full keyword list, it is time to make use of it and go after the attention of search engines. This is principally achieved through content – the information and material that comprise the pages of your website. Pages on your website that are optimized for SEO keywords are known as **SEO landing pages**. These pages contain structure content that is crafted around topical relevance to specific target keywords.

SEO best practices avoid optimizing a page for more than one keyword. This is not to say that you cannot have content that contains multiple keywords, but you should relegate these as secondary targets. There are two primary reasons for this. First, all web pages have a singular title, which is a major component in how search engines index pages. Well-written page titles are unlikely to be able to properly accommodate multiple key terms. The second reason is one of organization and analysis. As you track keyword performance, you want as little ambiguity and "bleed" between your data points. Every important keyword deserves its own specific focus. When keywords have their own dedicated pages, you can more easily track your SEO keyword efficacy and make more meaningful changes as needed.

If your website contains an online store, your first step in keyword content optimization is with your product listings. If you did your keyword research right, your products should have a selection of relevant key terms to target. Ensure that your product listings are dense with these keywords in the copy.

As with product listing pages, there are other "standard" web pages that you can optimize for keywords. Nearly every commercial or business website has "about" page(s). These are ideal pages to optimize your content around your brand keywords.

When creating content, remember this important rule: write the content for your audience but optimize it for the search engines. Any content pages you create should be focused on one primary and one or two secondary keywords. The content needs to be useful to your audience and ultimately serve to compel them to stay on your site on their journey toward a desired outcome. At the same time, the content must have the right mix and frequency of keywords to indicate to search engines that the page is relevant to the subject matter. This is known as **keyword density** and refers ratio of a keyword against the total words on a page. Keyword density requires a delicate balance, as too little tells the search engine it is not as relevant to the subject. If your keyword density is too high, a search engine may see this as a red flag and suspect your site of a practice called **keyword stuffing**. Keyword stuffing refers to the act of filling a page up with redundant repeating keywords in an attempt to fool the search crawler into thinking a low-quality webpage contains relevant content. Balancing keyword density with good, relevant content can be tricky. The ability to do so marks the difference between competent and incompetent search content marketers.

The Long Game

Search engine optimization and keyword marketing is an ongoing process. You need to be always playing the long game. When choosing which keywords target, begin with the most relevant to your products, industry, and brand. Once those are underway, you can move on to narrow and niche keywords. Never forget that no target keyword will ever be "done" in terms of targeting and optimization – you will always have to update and create new content. Search engines pay attention to not only keyword density, but also how often sites are updated with relevant content. "Stale" content often falls by the wayside in search results. In addition, the competitive landscape for search is always shifting. What works well for you today is not guaranteed to work tomorrow.

A surprisingly under looked fact about SEO is that search engines rank web *pages* and not *websites*. Some misguided SEOs will create multiple redundant and interlinked webpages within a website expecting increase search ranking for the entire site. This is not how search works and is why search results pages return links to relevant web pages, not domains. Having multiple pages serving the same keyword is a double-edged sword. On one hand, a website offering an abundance of content around a subject can be great for your visitors. However, you need to be concerned with something known as **keyword cannibalization**. This is a situation in which multiple pages on your website are competing with one another for search engine ranking. The Google algorithm also tends to limit how many search results come from a single web domain. Hence, your pages will not only be competing with other sites but can also dilute each other's ranking in the process. The solution to this conundrum is to merge cannibalizing pages together or even eliminate some of them to clear the field. If you want to avoid this issue in the first place, focus your keyword strategy on as few high-quality content pages as possible.

Avoiding cannibalization also helps you ward off another search engine pitfall: duplicate content. Unscrupulous search marketers will often take shortcuts and duplicate their content pages – often just swapping keywords for other keywords and calling it a day. From a user perspective, a site in which content is redundant from page to page is uncompelling. Search engines view this as both unhelpful for users and an attempt at "spamming" the algorithm with thinly veiled attempts to increase search ranking. In either case, search engines will penalize the rankings of such pages. In particularly egregious instances, search engines might even punish the entire web domain. The lesson here is simple: do not take shortcuts in SEO as the consequences can be crippling.

The Specter of PageRank

No discussion of SEO would be complete (or even minimally competent) without covering pagegank. **Pagerank** is a part of the Google search algorithm that measures the importance or "authority" of a webpage. Every page is assigned a "score" denoting its pagerank. This was once expressed on a scale of 0 to 10 back during a time when Google openly published pageranks. This scale was a simplification - the actual pagerank scale they use internally is much larger. In any case, the higher the pagerank score, the more authoritative it is. This scale is logarithmic, which means the distance between higher pagerank scores are further than between lower scores – it takes much more to move from 8 to 9 than it does 2 to 3.

Pagerank is determined primarily by the quantity and quality of links going to and from webpages. These links are treated as "votes" for the destination page. The idea is that a more authoritative site will have more votes from external websites than others. Not only is this considered a metric for topical authority, but also how trustworthy the site is. It is reasoned that people are less likely to link to questionable websites than credible ones.

Pagerank is not as simple as a matter of who gets the most links to their webpages. In fact, the algorithm itself is quite complicated, and is designed to prevent search rankings from being little more than a spam competition. Votes from webpages are not created equal. A link from a high-pagerank page carries much more weight than a link from a low rank page. The more authoritative the webpage, the more valuable their links are. A single link from an authoritative page is worth much more than multiple links from low-authority pages.

If you have a webpage with solid pagerank, you have a valuable SEO tool at your disposal. There is power in links from these pages, as a vote from them will help increase the pagerank of the destination page. While Google claims external linking has no effect on the origin pagerank, most SEO experts advise that you avoid excessive outward links.

High rank pages can help increase the overall rank of other webpages on the site. This is principally effectuated by effective site design with a unified navigation structure. If you have collections of pages of similar relevance, be sure to link to them from your high ranked pages. Failure to do this is a waste of the voting power your ranked pages possess. Again, as with every other aspect of SEO, there is a nuance to how often you should do this.

Pagerank and Back Again

Back in the day, search engine optimization may as well been called pagerank optimization. It dominated the SEO landscape for years. Much of this came about thanks to Google publishing site pageranks through their SEO research tools. Undoubtedly, they thought they were helping SEOs by providing this information. Unfortunately, this turned the entire industry on its head. As SEO is often a mad rush to divine the inner workings of search algorithms and then exploit them, it ushered in a flood of poor SEO practices. Link farms, link exchanges, link spamming, paid reciprocal links, and worse were rampant during this time.

Today, pagerank is still a big factor in how the Google algorithm works. However, as it is now discreet, SEOs rely on other metrics for page authority – particularly those furnished by third party services like SEMrush. However, these are at best educated guesses as to what the actual pageranks are for websites and should be treated as such.

Content is King, but Backlinks Rule

This all comes full circle to the current trend in search engine optimization: good content and quality **backlinks**. A backlink is a fancy term for links that come to your website from other sites. They are sometimes also called **inbound links**. The distinction with these links is that they are coming from pages and sources that you do not own or control. A link from one page on your website to another one on the same site is not a backlink.

Even without considering pagerank, you should understand why inbound links are so critical to SEO and website promotion in general. If your site has information that is useful and relevant, people will want to link to it. Good content is a principal way to entice these links, and so promoting your content is important. See Chapter 14 for more details.

Inbound links bring a many benefits to your website. For newer or inconspicuous websites, more links mean more avenues for search crawlers to find your site. Recall that search crawlers surf the web and follow links around the internet. If visitors can surf to your site, chances are a crawler can too. Understand that even if a search engine visits your site, if might not index it. This usually happens for new, low-content, or low-inbound link sites. More links means an increased likelihood of getting indexed. Finally, links simply bring in more visitors to your site – the very purpose weblinks were created for.

Write content for your human audience. Format content for your robot audience.

Chapter 9: Search Engine Optimization, Part 2

Technical SEO

In a perfect world, optimizing for search would begin and end simply with great content. Though search algorithms are getting smarter every day, they still need help "seeing" the entirety of your website and the pages that comprise it. This brings us to the technical side of SEO and website design. This stuff is not advanced computer science, but does requires a modest level of technical knowhow. If you can afford it, you still might consider involving a developer in this stage of SEO. However, you should still get yourself a basic grasp of how it all works – it makes working with technical people more pleasant and cost effective.

Websites and search engines are software, and so they must be approached accordingly. The fundamental technical considerations for SEO include site navigability, structure, URL formatting, source code, and metadata. Additionally, a site is not truly optimized for search unless it is fast-loading and mobile-friendly. It's a lot to consider, but not unsurmountable by a small team or even an individual.

Site Navigation and Structure

To best accommodate human visitors and search crawlers alike, a well-organized site structure is essential. This involves both up-front page navigation and backend file structure. Despite the very different nature of a human user and an AI search bot, you can apply much the same paradigms for accommodating both.

All navigational links on your site need to be represented as text. Search crawlers cannot read text contained in images or video media. You also want to avoid having your navigational elements hidden behind interactive menus or popups. Primary navigation should be as technologically rudimentary as possible and be present at the same location on every page in your site. This practice both serves visitors consistent navigation and removes all barriers for crawlers to assess your site pages and directory structure.

Your website should be organized in a flat, hierarchical manner. This organization must be reflected in the navigational elements on every page in the site. A **hierarchical structure** means that as you link deeper into the site, pages follow a clear path of greater focus and specificity for each top-level topic. The home page of should be a general directory of the overall website. The first-level links should lead to general category pages, and each link within those go into deeper specificity to that category.

A **flat site structure** is one where all pages within the site should be within a few link levels of one another. This means that while your site is laid out in a hierarchical manner, keeping to a flat structure means minimizing how deep and specific this hierarchy is. Do not go overboard on granularity for the sake of it – the deepest pages in your hierarchy should be no more than three of four clicks away from your homepage.

One paradigm for organizing your website pages is the concept of organizing content into **silos**. A silo is a vertical organizational structure in which your top-level pages are broad-term landing pages. Each successive layer of sub-pages are more specific offshoots of the main topic. These sub-pages in turn might link to further sub-pages for even more specific topics. Siloed pages are organized to be separate and isolated from unrelated topics of the same or deeper levels. Siloed content structure is particularly useful if your site contains a large number of topics or products.

Navigational Breadcrumbs

Best SEO practices hold that you should have breadcrumb navigation on all pages in the site. **Breadcrumbs** are those horizontal lists of pages at the top of sites indicating your location on the site in relation to its navigational hierarchy. For example: Home > Beer > Coors > Coors Light. This not only makes for easier navigation for visitors, but it also ensures cross-linking between related pages and easier crawling for bots.

URL and Directory Structure

In a manner like your site structure, your website URLs should follow a unified structure. URLs should adhere to a consistent structure across the entire site regardless of the type of content on the pages. In addition, URLs should be human readable and make logical sense to anyone looking at them. They should also be descriptive and should reflect the page title or product name, if applicable. Most website platforms have URL configuration settings that let you easily set yours to follow these rules.

Effectively designed websites have well organized internal directory structures. This means that the files and folders that comprise your site are not placed on your web server in a jumbled manner. Not only does this make site maintenance easier, but it also makes it easier to manage your URL structure and further optimize it for search crawlers. The URL structure of a website often follows the internal file directory structure on the backend the website. If this is the case for you, then most of this work is done for you already.

Your Source Code

Good source code is easier to manage for programmers and better for search engine crawlers to navigate. Search engines are getting better than ever at reading and deciphering the content of websites. However, they still are far from perfect and have trouble reading certain types of page elements. Your source code must be accommodating to crawlers as much as possible. You want to minimize any hindrances on your site that might affect search engine bots.

The first part of optimizing your code base is to ensure you are using as little uncrawlable code as possible. Crawlability is so important to web development that it effectively killed the Adobe Flash platform. These days, you will likely have to deal with javascript and its issues with search. **Javascript** is one of the principal technologies on which the modern internet is based. It is immensely useful for creating websites with interactive or dynamic elements. It enables a user to interact with the page and make changes without it having to call back home to the server and reload the page.

While the dynamic nature of javascript makes it great for website usability, it can create problems for search engines. Web crawlers do not interact with dynamic pages in the way a human would. In addition, javascript code might contain elements and information that is not rendered in the actual displayed page. Due to the ubiquity of javascript, search crawlers are becoming increasingly better at reading it. Generally, they try to render and read javascript webpages in the same way a human visitor would. The results have been mostly positive, but there are still several issues and concerns regarding javascript and search. The best course of action for search-optimized webpages is to use it sparingly. When you are using javascript, ensure that it is rendering properly for and not disrupting search bots.

Metadata

Search engines do more than view webpages as they are seen by human visitors – they read sites at the code level. There is an entire realm of additional page information visible to search crawlers below the surface. This is known as **metadata,** and as the term suggests, is data that describes data. For webpages, metadata provides additional information about the content and page elements within. In the simplest cases, metadata will indicate what type of information or content is present in a page element. In more complex usage, metadata provides full descriptions about the content on the webpage, its keywords, and how crawlers should treat links.

Metadata is expressed in web source code using **tags**. Tags are short pieces of text contained within brackets that indicate the identity, start, end, and contents of the metadata element. The descriptive metadata itself is contained within these tags.

See the following example:

<title>Drywall repair: You can learn to fix it by yourself</title>

<meta name="description" content="All about how you can repair drywall by yourself" />

<meta name="keywords" content="drywall repair, drywall fix, diy drywall repair" />

The first line in the code above is the all-important "title" tag. This is the most basic and essential piece of metadata for all webpages. Note that the title information itself is nested between an opening and closing title tag. These tags bracket the title content, telling the search crawler where the title begins and where it ends.

The next two lines describe two other types of metadata. First, the tag is declared as being a metatag with the "meta" descriptor at the front. Next, the name of the metatag is provided. The next element is the actual content – in these cases being the page description and the keywords. Finally, the end of the metadata is declared with a closing "/>" tag. (Note: the example "keywords" tag is rarely used by search crawlers anymore.)

There are many types of metadata tags in HTML, but there are a few that are indispensable for SEO. These are tags that should be implemented on every page on your website that you are trying to optimize for search. The following list outlines the metadada you should be principally concerned with:

Title Tag

The **title tag** is the first and foremost element on a webpage that describes the page title. It is often what search engines use as the headline when listing search results. Web browsers also use the title tag when displaying a page on a browser tab.

Description Tag

As seen in the previous code example, the **description tag** provides a brief description of the content on the webpage. Aside from informing search engines about your content, the description tag is principally used to populate the site description that appears below search results titles. The description tag should therefore be written in a manner that entices visitors to click to your site.

Headings

Heading tags are used to identify various levels of headings in your content. These should be structured in the same way as you would any text blocking content: Broad topics split into more specific sub-topics. Heading levels are denoted by numbers: <h1>, <h2>, <h3>, and so on. Not only do heading tags promote good organization, but they also help search crawlers better understand your content.

Alt Tags

Search Crawlers cannot read images, and so rely on metadata to determine their content. This is handled by the **alt tag**, which is embedded into the image HTML tag. In addition, you can further ensure your image content is being "seen" by search engines by including captions under every image on your page.

Alt tags are also important for the accessibility of your webpages to visually impaired visitors. The software they use to parse websites for them relies on these tags to determine image content.

Schema Markup

Although search engines are getting progressively smarter, they still have a long way to go in determining the content of most websites perfectly. This is why tags and metadata continue to be important in SEO work. To further aid search engines to understand page content, they have been increasingly reliant on **schema markup**.

Schema markup is a form of **structured data** – information that is stored in a distinct data field within a file. It is a framework for properly declaring and defining specific information on a webpage. Basically, schema markup is information placed in your website source code that describes the page content in a way that search engines can quickly and clearly understand. Schema markup is typically placed in the header code elements of a site but can go just about anywhere.

Below is an example of a very simple schema for a blog article, as it would be posted within the source code of that page:

```
{
  "@context" : "http://schema.org",
  "@type" : "Article",
  "name" : "The Martial Way",
  "author" : {
    "@type" : "Person",
    "name" : "Gregory Shefler"
  },
  "datePublished" : "2021-08-23T11:30",
}
```

Breaking down the example above, we see that it is essentially a list of data. The first part declares what the data is, and the next part is the data itself. The name of the article is "The Martial Way" and it was written by a person named Gregory Shefler on August 23, 2021. Notice that the author information contains a nested list inside its own brackets. This allows for the possibility that the type of author, declared by "@type", might not be a person but an organization or group.

As you can see, structured data markup is not overly complicated, but it does require minor technical legwork to do right. How do you know what data types and names to use? **Schema.org** is an initiative created by the major search engines and acts as a central hub for all schema rules. This website is a searchable repository of every data type and how to declare them in your schema. Though there are multiple structured data frameworks, you should focus primarily on the one Google recommends: **JSON-LD**.

Though schema markup is not a requirement for SEO, it is rapidly becoming a standard practice and should be included in your content strategy. Though it is not rocket science, it can be a bit complicated and tedious depending on your website. Fortunately, there are tools that make the creation of markup schema much easier. Many website platforms have started offering automatic schema creation as features. These tools work just fine, though they still sometimes need some manual tweaks to be optimally effective.

Sitemaps

Whether you are visiting a website or a city, having a map is always useful. **Sitemaps** are just what they sound like: maps of the content and layout of a website. Having a sitemap has been a staple of web design for a long time and for good reason – it helps visitors find the pages they are looking for in a single, easy-to-read location. And just as you have both human and AI visitors to your website, so too should you have sitemaps to accommodate each.

Sitemaps intended for human visitors are best placed in two locations on your pages. The footer element at the bottom of your site is the most common location for an abridged sitemap outlining the most popular/relevant pages for most visitors. Depending on the size of your site, this placement might be all you need. Larger sites or those with more complex content structure would do well to have a dedicated page for a full sitemap. These are best laid out in a standard outline format employing purely textual links and nothing fancy.

Sitemaps are essential to proper SEO. The most common and versatile way of doing so is with *XML* **sitemaps**. These are sitemaps written in a markup format called XML. **XML** stands for *Extensible Markup Language*. In this protocol, data is described in bracketed beginning and ending tags with the data contained within. This is not unlike schema markups, though it is generally less complicated. The beauty of XML sitemaps is that you can describe pages in your site with additional information for search engines aside from just the URLs. For example, you can tell them how often the pages are updated or when they were last modified.

Thanks to their ubiquity, creating XML sitemaps is relatively easy. There is a plethora of online tools that can auto-generate a sitemap for your website. Additionally, most website platforms today have built-in sitemap generators. The tradeoff is that these sitemaps tend to be very basic and do not contain the more granular information described previously. XML sitemaps should have their own dedicated URL location. Most typically, they are placed on websites along the lines of "https://www.my-website/sitemap.xml".

Directing Search Engines

There are times when your SEO tactics require you to provide special instructions to search crawlers. Though you typically want search engines to crawl and index as many of your webpages as possible, there are exceptions. For instance, private pages like user account or checkout pages are neither beneficial or secure to be indexed. There are also times when you do not want a crawler to follow an external link on your website. The common scenario for this is for when you do not want your link to be a "vote" to the destination site that increases their pagerank.

The Robots Metatag

The **robots meta tag** is placed in the header of a webpage and can provide instructions to search bots. These instructions can include whether to index the page; if the bot should follow links or not; if it can provide a snippet in search results pages; or even an expiration date on indexing the page. There are other commands available too, but not all search bots obey all the same rules. The robots meta tag can also provide instructions to all search crawlers or even just specific ones.

Robots.txt

The **robots.txt** is a file that can exist on the home directory of your website. It is similar in functionality to the robots meta tag but applies globally to the entire site. This file lets you tell search bots if there are any directories or pages on your site that they are not allowed to crawl or index. You do not want search bots to access or index certain pages or directories such as private pages, duplicate content, or script directories. Robots.txt is where you place the list of these pages and directories and instruct search bots how they should treat them.

Mobile-First Search

The latter half of the 2010s saw the bulk of internet traffic shift away from desktop computers toward mobile devices. By the

2020s, more than half of all internet traffic was on mobile devices and this trend continues upward. To accommodate this shift, Google adapted its systems to prioritize the mobile versions of sites. This is known as **mobile-first indexing**, where the mobile view of a webpage is used for indexing and ranking. Though it took several years to enact, mobile-first indexing has largely become the standard for all online search.

It you don't have a mobile-friendly website, you are at a tremendous disadvantage from both an SEO and human usability standpoint. There are two principal ways in which a website may be mobile-ready. The first is to maintain a separate mobile version of your site. The issue here is that it creates extra work since it requires you to maintain two websites rather than one. The best way to maintain a mobile-friendly site is by using **responsive design**. A responsive website will automatically adjust itself to the device it is viewed on. This is achieved through adaptive programming, scaling, and styling on the site. Fortunately, the pervasiveness of mobile in the internet landscape has made it easier than ever to create mobile-friendly websites. Every website platform worth its salt has automatic functionality to accommodate mobile devices. Even with this relative ease, you will need to ensure your mobile views have complete functional and/or content parity with the desktop view – or risk ranking penalties from search engines.

Core Web Vitals: The Need for Speed

Google has continually been shifting its search algorithms to regard user experience as a ranking factor. It is no longer enough to have relevant content – your site needs to perform well too. This initiative is known as **Core Web Vitals**. As a measure of user experience, Core Web Vitals is ultimately a measure of speed. The faster a website loads and renders, the better. Of course, a fast-loading site that is a chore to navigate is still going to have issues with ranking. However, when all other factors are equal, Google will prioritize faster websites over their peers.

Core Web Vitals measures three elements of the loading/rendering process of a webpage. The first is called **Largest Contentful Paint**, which is the speed at which the main content of a page has loaded. The next is the **First Input Delay** and assesses the speed at which interactive page elements have loaded – the earlies point at which users can click or interact with the page. Finally, there is the **Cumulative Layout Shift**. This is how much the final render of the webpage differs from the rest of the page load time. Undoubtedly you have experienced a webpage where, a few seconds after loading, every element on the page suddenly shifts to accommodate an ad or other content. This is the behavior Cumulative Layout Shift measures for.

It was always important to have a fast website, but Core Web Vitals has turned it into an SEO necessity. Page speed can be hindered by numerous factors including poor server performance; low internet bandwidth; poorly optimized website software; or even outdated user hardware/software. If your website is a poor Core Web Vitals performer, you will need to determine exactly what the issue is and respond accordingly. You can evaluate your Core Web Vitals by using the free **Google Search Console** toolset.

Local Search

Businesses or organizations with local reach must contend with another layer of SEO – local search. Local reach means that your target audience and/or customers are in a specific geographic region. Contending with local search is both a blessing and a curse. For one thing, the search competition is much narrower in scope and your target audience is much more geographically specific. However, depending on your market and area, the competition between a small group of businesses for a small group of potential customers can be fierce.

The most direct way to target locally is a matter of selecting the right local keywords. This type of keyword is known as a **geo-targeted keyword**. These keywords identify a geographic location, such as a town, street, locale, area, region, or even an address. These keywords are as essential to a local business as their brand, market, and persona keywords. After all, what good is attracting visitors to your website if they all live too far from your location to become a potential customer?

As the largest search engine, your local business must have a **Google Business Profile** account – previously known as **Google MyBusiness**. It lets you claim ownership of a business online where you can input your company information. This includes addresses, hours, phone numbers, contact info, and more. In exchange, Google will display your business information for relevant local search results. Additionally, it enables users to leave reviews of your business for others to see. Many prospective customers rely on reviews when choosing products and services, and so this is essential. Finally, it gives you access to analytical tools that provide information on how often people search for and view your business.

Image Search

Once broadband and fast wireless networks became standard, image searches became increasingly common. Today, all search engines provide images as part of their search results pages. Depending on the query, images can appear as elements on the main search results page. Furthermore, search engines allow for image-specific search results in their queries. Image search is an often-overlooked opportunity for boosting organic traffic. Image results not only display relevant images, but they provide links to the webpage from where they originate. Unlike normal search results pages, users are more likely to scroll further on an image search. This provides further opportunities for your images to drive traffic to your site. Better yet, if you are a retailer, your product images can lead directly to your product listing pages.

Optimizing your images for search is principally a matter of following best practices tagging the images on your site. Your image filenames and alt metatags should be clearly descriptive of their content. Images on your site should have identifying captions below them as well. For these elements, be sure to utilize your target keywords – you are optimizing your images for the same algorithm that ranks webpages. These keywords should be the same ones that the page on which the image resides is optimized for. Speaking of keywords, your images will not rank in image results if the pages they reside on are not search keyword optimized. Search engines ultimately determine the relevance of an image based on the content of the page on which it resides.

You can further bolster your image search optimization using structured data markup. This provides search engines with additional information on the content of your images. The more descriptive elements you can provide to search, the better it can understand your content. Remember to utilize your relevant keywords in your markup as well.

SEO Shenanigans

Whether you do your own SEO, hire someone, or outsource it completely, beware of the dark side. Since its inception, Search Engine Optimization has been rife with scams, unethical practices, shady characters, and outright cheaters. Since search engine providers have an incentive to keep their algorithms secret, much of the practice of SEO is constantly trying to figure out how they work. This ambiguity has enabled many contradictory and false claims about SEO. Charlatans thrive in these conditions, as they can make brash claims about what they know about search and how they can help you rank "guaranteed number one on all the search engines".

The SEO business, or "community", is often split into two paradigms: white-hat and black-hat. **White hat SEO** generally comprise the "good" practices that are ethical, follow the rules, and are on the up-and-up with search providers. **Black hat SEO** constitutes the shady and unethical side. Black hat tactics might increase the search performance of a page, but only because it exploits and manipulates the algorithms. These tactics nearly always violate search engines terms of service. Sites caught using these tactics run the risk of ranking penalties or outright bans from the search index. Some SEOs recognize a third variety of SEO that exploits the search algorithms but not *quite* as unethically. This gray area is appropriately referred to as **grey-hat SEO**.

Despite the promises from their unscrupulous practitioners, black-hat SEO is not worth it. The penalties for running afoul of search engines are severe and can outright destroy a website. Some of these practices include:

Keyword Stuffing

Keyword stuffing is a practice that overpopulates, or "stuffs" webpages full of the same target keywords repeatedly. Proper keyword-dense content do indeed reuse key terms, but with relevance to the content. Stuffed keyword content is redundancy for the sake of it and can result in harsh search penalties. This is one of the oldest and easily thwarted black hat tactics.

Misuse of Schema Markup

Black hat SEOs will sometimes place misleading or outright false schema markup data on their pages. The intent is to falsely bolster the content of the page in the eyes of the search engine. Also, search result pages that include page descriptions and snippets often use schema markup to populate them. Misused schema markup will thus taint the search results page with incorrect information – something search engines work to avoid.

Link Farms and Blog Link Networks

A **link farm** is a webpage that exists solely to host a bunch of links but with little or no original content. They are created specifically to create a large number of backlinks to the site practicing black-hat SEO.

As link farms fell out of favor once search engines became privy to the practice, black-hat SEOs moved to **blog link networks**. These are interrelated blogs and content sites that appear to be independent but are operated by black-hat SEOs. These blogs will post content and links all pointing to the site they are trying to boost. This falsely creates the appearance of a well-linked authoritative site, and thus would unfairly boost its pagerank.

Spam Commenting

In nearly every blog comment section or online forum, you will see one-off commenters posting links to some external site. This is an example of a spam comment. They are attempting to create links within a large and/or high authority website to boost traffic and ranking for the target sites.

Cloaking

Cloaked websites pull bait-and-switch maneuvers with search engines. These sites will show search crawlers one version of the webpage but a completely different one to human visitors. This is most often used to hide unscrupulous content from search engines.

Buying and Selling Links

Pagerank is built upon the idea that good content will be frequently linked to. For a website with trust or authority to link to a "smaller" site, it likely means the site contains relevant content. Black-hat SEOs partake in the practice of buying and selling links to improperly exploit the system. Obviously, this harms the intent and efficacy of the pagerank system. Google does not look (or act) kindly upon buying and selling links and will penalize accordingly.

Final Words

Search engine optimization is neither alchemy nor rocket science. Since search algorithms are ever-changing and veiled in secrecy, it is inherently imprecise and often vague. Conversely, SEO is an exercise in best practices for both online content creation and web technology. Search optimization is just that: optimization. By following the current best state of right practices and guidelines as provided by Google and other search providers, you will have already gone a long way in ensuring your site can be all it can be in search ranking. SEO continues as an unending process of learning about the latest guidelines and practices and implementing them. Just as a website is a garden, SEO is a practice not unlike periodic weeding or pruning – it never ends and is always necessary.

The first rule of SEO is that you can always do it better.

Chapter 10: Paid Search, Part 1

The other side of search marketing is paid search, colloquially known as **PPC**, or **pay per click**. The major search engines are not charities, and their primary business model is to serve paid advertising. Search companies are playing a constant balancing game: they want to maximize ad revenue, but if their organic search results are seen as unreliable, fewer people will trust them enough to use the search engine in the first place. Search providers have navigated this balancing act well enough, though in some cases, they have blurred the lines between how paid and organic search results appear. In your online marketing strategy, you should utilize both paid and organic search – regardless of your relative success at either. Many search users do not know or care about the difference between paid or organic results, and so you must cater to everyone. Also, just as organic search algorithms change, so does the competitive environment for paid search. Optimizing for both is essential.

Pay per click (PPC) is precisely what it sounds like –you pay the search platform every time someone clicks on ads that you create. Every major search platform offers PPC advertising, with Google far being the juggernaut. For the remainder of this chapter, we will be focusing on the Google PPC platform. The reason is twofold: first, Google dominates search to such a degree that you absolutely *must* utilize and optimize for it. Second, the other search PPC platforms behave in much the same way as Google, and nearly every feature on Google has an analogue on the others. Though there are nuances to different search platforms, Google ultimately sets the stage in how they function for both paid and organic search.

How Paid Search Works

Just as Google ranks organic results based on keywords (amongst other factors), Google Ads serves paid placements based on these same keywords. The Google Ads platform, like most PPC solutions, is built upon an auction model. Advertisers place bids against one another toward their desired target keywords. When a search query with the relevant keywords is run, Google will serve ads on the search results page with the highest bidders on top – if your bids are too low, you might not even have your ad appear at all. If a search user clicks on your ad, Google will get paid what you agreed to bid for the ad – hence the term "pay per click". Upon clicking, the paid ad leads the visitor to the destination page as set by you, the advertiser.

With PPC, there is a stark difference between the objectives of the advertiser and Google. Google gets paid whenever somebody clicks on an ad, period. However, as the advertiser, you do not generate revenue based on who clicks your ads. You make money only when and if the visitor takes the appropriate actions to convert into a paid customer. In most cases, this is part of a larger marketing funnel. Hence, the clicks you pay for is an investment in the visitor in the hopes they convert into a customer.

Though you are competing against other ad bidders in PPC, your primary adversary is the conflict of interest between you and Google. They design their system to maximize clicks. You must design your PPC marketing strategy to focus on maximizing *quality* clicks. This means taking measures to ensure your ads appear only to the audience most likely to convert into customers. One hundred quality visitors are worth more than one thousand low-quality visitors.

Same as it Never Was – The Changing Landscape of PPC

As the internet changes with time, technology, and culture, so does the nature of online advertising. The 2010s saw a renewed concern with privacy and data security on the internet. This was propelled by the continuing growth of giant web companies and the dominance of social media. For this chapter, it would be negligent not to mention some of the recent changes in the online ad space.

The most potentially far-ranging change emerging on the internet has to do with privacy. The manner and scope in how users are tracked by private and public entities is falling under increasing scrutiny. This is what spurred the creation of legislation such as **GDPR**, or the **General Data Protection Regulation**. This far-reaching legislation passed by the EU set the stage for a global wave of similar rules and regulations regarding the collection and use of personal data. One notable example is the California Consumer Privacy Act (CCPA). Such policies will likely become normalized in the coming decade.

The current and upcoming changes in how people can be tracked online have direct consequences in how online advertising will be conducted. Google has already begun phasing out certain aspects of its PPC targeting. For example, targeting users based on their browsing history will be diminished, if not eliminated. In addition, targeting ads based on user's devices or directly in their online messages will be changed or removed.

Google is currently in the midst of a major upheaval in this space, by virtually eliminating 3rd party cookies online (their Chrome web browser dominates the internet). These cookies have been used to track online users and extrapolate huge amounts of data about their interests and buying tendencies. This data has always been of immense value to advertisers. The elimination of this aspect of online tracking will necessitate new ways to target online ads. Google is working on a replacement, known as **Federated Learning of Cohorts**, or **FLoC**. This AI-based approach hopes to maintain ad targeting value while preserving individual users' privacy. Time will tell if this specific solution works out. In any case, it portends a major paradigm shift in how online ads will work in the future.

The Importance of Landing Pages

Enticing someone to click through on one of your ads is only part of the path to converting them into customers. Your ad must take them to a place that will further motivate them to continue their customer journey. This is where the importance of your landing pages comes in. **Landing pages** are the destination webpages your ads link to. They must be specifically relevant to the content of the ad they are linked to. People have very little tolerance if they feel they have clicked on a link that takes them somewhere irrelevant or unexpected.

If you are just starting out with a website, PPC landing pages should be as important a consideration in planning as your SEO keyword pages. In many cases, as you are sharing much the same selection of target keywords, SEO and PPC landing pages can be the same. However, the types of keywords you will target in PPC will be narrower in terms of desired calls-to-action by visitors. In these cases, you would best be crafting separate pages for PPC and SEO.

Though PPC is primarily about ads and bids on keywords, Google does look at your landing pages when factoring a metric known as the **Quality Score**. Quality Score is a part of the Google search ads algorithm that quantifies the relevance between your target keywords, ad copy, and landing page. This is measured on a scale of 1-10 and, unlike pagerank, is viewable to the advertiser on the Google Ads dashboard. The intent of Quality Score is to incentivize ads that are most relevant to search queries. Quality Score is important but beware that it primarily serves Googles' objective to maximize clicks, not conversions. Do not sacrifice your conversion rate for a higher click rate, even if it means taking a hit to your Quality Score.

Knowing Ad Placement Types

Google Ads is comprised of two separate advertising networks. The primary network is the search network, which serves relevant ads on search engine results pages (SERPs) along with traditional organic results. The other network is the display network. This network comprises advertising that gets placed on various websites around the internet as embedded elements on webpages. The display network comprises many popular sites, including the video giant YouTube.

The biggest distinction between the search and display networks has to do with user motivations. When someone is using a search engine, they are specifically looking for information. If your ads are relevant to their search keywords, it can get served to them in the results pages. Your ads appear in front of users looking for your type of webpage content. In contrast, display ads display in places where the user is browsing a webpage the ad is served on. Users browsing websites are not in an active search mindset. These users are not there to see your ads, they are interested in the content of the page they are looking at.

Most businesses should initially avoid the display network and focus on search. The targeting of the ads on search is an infinitely better return on investment (ROI) proposition when compared to the display network. The display network is a better fit for branding and mindshare building campaigns.

Keywords, Negative Keywords, and Search Terms

PPC ads are based around bidding on search keywords. These are much the same keywords that you would target for in your SEO efforts, which is why the Google Keyword Planner tool can be used for both purposes. Just as with keywords and SEO, the more competitive a keyword is, the more competition there is in bidding to get your ads to appear. This also factors in how the cost per click is calculated. Expect to pay high prices for clicks on highly competitive keywords.

An important distinction between targeting keywords for SEO vs. PPC is how keywords are utilized. For SEO, your webpages will have to include the keywords you are targeting for ranking. The content of the destination webpage is what determines whether it will show up in search results or not. With PPC, your ad copy and the keywords you are targeting are separate. While it is advisable you use keywords in your ad copy to make it more clickable to the user, its presence there does not determine placement. Writing proper PPC ad copy will be covered later in Chapter 11.

As with SEO, you should target long-tail keywords and phrases in your PPC efforts. Recall that long-tail keywords are bulks of less-competitive keywords related to "bigger" competitive keywords. In aggregate, these keywords comprise significant potential audiences while maintaining lower costs to bid on.

One of the most important concepts in PPC marketing is the use of **negative keywords**. Negative keywords are keywords that you utilize to exclude your ads from being displayed. For instance, if you are looking to advertise your non-fiction reference book about martial arts, you would do best to ensure your ads do not come up for users searching for martial arts fiction. Hence, your negative keywords would include terms like "fiction", "fantasy", "stories", and the like. Any searches for martial arts books that have these negative terms will be excluded from your ad placements. Furthermore, you want to prevent people who are looking for freebies from wasting your ad budget. To this end, your negative keywords would be terms such as "free", "for free", and "giveaway". In these examples, you have just prevented a huge number of irrelevant clicks and saved money.

Negative keywords are essential tools in crafting PPC campaigns around receptive target audiences. By crafting your keyword strategy with the right mix of targeted keywords and exclusionary negative keywords, you are optimizing for search queries. Remember: though you bid for ad placements via keywords, your overall campaigns should be optimized for search terms.

Targeting Competitors

Targeting a competitors' names, brands, and trademarks in your PPC campaigns is far less murky than targeting them for SEO. This is even less problematic for trademarked terms because you can target them as PPC keywords without having to use them in your ad copy. Competitor keywords are generally less competitive to bid for than other terms. Depending on the size or uniqueness of these keywords, they are deeply focused on a narrow target audience. As competitors, they should be driving the same target audience. Having your ads come up in search for competitors also helps you build mindshare with search users as another name in the industry, niche, or subject matter.

Going after competitor keywords is not always a slam-dunk for success. For one thing, if someone is searching specifically for your competitor by name or brand, then they are likely to be singularly motivated to find them. In most cases, this would result in comparatively few clicks on your ads. In addition, some visitors might click on your ad thinking it was your competitor. This could create anger toward your business if they see this as a deception. Finally, some businesses are very territorial regarding their branded PPC turf – especially for terms that they go through the trouble and expense of trademarking. If you decide to target competitors in the way, do not be shocked if you receive missives from lawyers or even have them target *your* brand and trademarks. Targeting competitors is not against Google terms of service, and so it comes down to your sense of professional courtesy and/or appetite for a fight.

Paid Search Performance Objectives

Before further discussing PPC strategy, it is important to understand the performance goals you want to achieve. Ultimately, your goals are congruous to your SEO strategy: to attract visitors to your website who are the most likely to convert into customers in a timely and cost-effective manner. Whereas SEO is focused on the long game by influencing search algorithms, PPC is much more immediate – you can start getting clicks to your site practically the moment your advertising account is established.

To properly understand PPC objectives, you need to know the associated concepts and lingo. Below is a list of some of the most common and important performance terminology:

Maximum Bid

Everything in paid search begins with how much you are willing to pay for someone to click on your ad. Advertisers compete for ad placement in an auction format for each keyword term they want to target. For each of these keywords, you will set your maximum bid. This is the maximum amount you are willing to pay to get a single click on your ad. More competitive keywords generally garner more potential traffic and thus require higher maximum bids.

Impressions

Impressions denote the number of times your ad has been seen (or was at least viewable) over a period of time. For instance, an ad with one thousand impressions means that it was displayed in search results one thousand times. On its own, impressions do not differentiate between different users, so several impressions might have been shown to the same person. Conversely, **unique impressions** refers to the number of individual users who have seen the ad.

Cost-Per-Thousand Impressions (CPM)

Your ads might not always display on searches you are trying to target. Google takes factors like ad quality, relevance, and click bids into account when determining which ads to serve. The CPM metric provides insight into how well your ads perform as they are served. Since you do not pay for search ads unless there are clicks, CPM is a measure of your click-throughs versus the number of instances the ad displayed.

Some ad networks, like the Google display network can charge by how many times an ad displays – regardless of if it gets clicked. In these cases, CPM is the most direct metric for to your ad costing. Recall that this type of ad strategy is best used for branding and mindshare building.

CTR: Click-Through-Rate

This is the metric that measures engagement users have with an ad. It is the ratio between the number of times people have clicked on your ad and the number of times it has been shown. For instance, an ad with 65 clicks and 250 impressions would have a CTR of 26 percent (65 ÷ 250).

Higher click-through rates generally suggest that the ad is more compelling to the people it is shown to. However, this is not the entire story in terms of PPC strategy. Your goal is to maximize clicks from people who are most likely to become paying customers. A high click rate is a waste of resources unless it is ultimately generating conversions.

Cost-Per-Click (CPC)

The costs of pay-per-click ads can be variable as they are determined by a bidding mechanism. The actual cost of a click is only finalized when the clickthrough has happened. This metric is an important one to track when determining your auction bidding strategy. Similarly, there is the **Average Cost-Per-Click (ACPC)** which represents the average price you are paying per click.

Conversion Rate

PPC campaigns live or die depending on their conversion rates. A **conversion** is counted every time a visitor takes the desired action of the ad campaign. A conversion is commonly defined as a sale, but it can describe just about any action the marketer has built their marketing campaign around achieving. The conversion rate is the ratio of conversions to ad clicks. So, an ad that got 100 clicks with 5 sales would have a 5 percent conversion rate.

Recall that the process of turning a stranger into a paying customer is not always instantaneous and involves a series of steps along the customer journey. Because of this, PPC platforms have time windows in which to count something as a conversion. By default, Google allows for a 30-day window after a clickthrough for a conversion to be counted. This means that if a customer clicks on an ad on November 1st and ultimately makes a purchase on November 20th, that initial click will be credited with the sale. Had the order taken place after 30 days, it would not have been counted against the initial click.

Cost-Per-Conversion

The cost-per-conversion measures the average of how much you paid per action. If you paid $100 to get 20 clicks and 5 of them converted, then your average cost per conversion was $20 (your cost-per-click was only $5 by comparison).

Cost-Per-Acquisition (CPA)

CPA is the average cost you incur to specifically convert a visitor into a paying customer. The reason this is often tracked as a separate metric has to do with buyer journeys and marketing funnels. There might be many intermediate steps between the fist click on a site to them becoming a paying customer. Both metrics need to be tracked to get a complete picture of your overall strategy.

Cost per acquisition is ultimately the cost it takes to obtain a paying customer. More customers mean more revenue, and this metric indicates the current investment necessary to increase that number. It both can indicate how much can be invested into further customer acquisition or whether your current PPC model is effectively creating new customers.

Return on Ad Spend (ROAS)

This metric is extremely important. It is the ratio between the revenue generated through click-through conversions and the total advertising spend. Naturally, you want this ratio to be as high as possible – especially if your revenue model is primarily based upon online sales. ROAS is the ultimate determinant of the sustainability of your search marketing efforts – if it is not making money to at least break even, it is not working. Such campaigns need either serious tweaking or total abandonment.

The Google Ads Hierarchy

The structure of Google Ads is hierarchical and represents the type of structure you will see on other advertising platforms. As with the other aspects of search marketing, Google's approach determines how the other platforms are structured. To newcomers, the Google Ads backend can seem quite intimidating. One of the biggest annoyances about the Google Ads setup is that it displays all components of the entire account regardless of the view. For instance, if you want to manage your keywords for only a single campaign ad group, you will have to drill past the keywords for every campaign in your account.

Cynically speaking, such a convoluted design might be a deliberate as Google has been increasingly pushing AI-managed ad management. If you have ever had the privilege of having a Google employee "help" optimize your Google Ads strategy, you will understand this sentiment. The more intimidating manual ad curation seems, the more people will choose to rely on Google's automation. Such automation will always favor maximizing clicks over conversions. Fortunately, the Google Ads hierarchy can be managed once you understand its structure.

Account

The highest level is the *account* level, or the *All Campaigns* view. This is your overall view of everything in your ads account and where you can access global settings and payment options.

Campaigns

The next level comprises all your individual ads campaigns. A Campaign is the umbrella under which your ads share a single budget, target network, geographic targets, and more. You can also set scheduling for your campaigns with distinct start and end dates. Campaigns should focus on a singular end goal for all ads that live under them. For instance, you would have one campaign dedicated to generating sales leads, another for direct online sales, and another for email newsletter signups.

Ad Groups

Ad Groups are groups of ads within a campaign. The best practice for grouping ads is for each one to focus on a single primary keyword and its variants. You can set your search ad bids at this level which will encompass all ads within.

Ads and Keywords

This is the most distinctive level of the PPC hierarchy. It is where your actual ad copy resides. It is also where you set your target keywords and negative keywords. Notably, you can set separate bid amounts at the keyword level too.

"Ovaltine? A crummy commercial?" – 'Ralphie', from A Christmas Story

---

Chapter 11: Paid Search, Part 2

<u>Doing Keywords Right</u>

To win with search marketing, you must play by the rules of the search engines. Both your paid search ads and your organically ranked search pages will be showing up in the same place – the search engine results page (SERP). Remember that search marketing is a holistic and synergistic process. Optimal search coverage comes through focusing on both the paid and organic sides of the equation. If you did proper keyword research for your SEO strategy, then you already have your primary keyword targets for PPC – refer to Chapter 8 if you need a refresher.

The principal difference between the keywords you target for PPC vs SEO concern your calls-to-action. Pages that rank well in organic search often retain their relative ranking positions outside of drastic events like a penalty or major algorithm change. Paid search ads will only show up if their campaigns are active and bidding competitively. Consequently, your paid ads must focus on keywords and phrases that evoke immediacy and are conducive to making someone click-through and convert. These are known as **Transactional Keywords**.

Transactional keywords comprise one of the three types of search queries. This first are **Navigational Queries**, in which users are looking for a specific website or entity. For example, someone looking for their nearest Starbucks will be searching along the lines of "Starbucks near me", "Starbucks official", or even just "Starbucks". The next type of query are **Informational Queries**, where the user is seeking information about a topic. This type of query is broad in scope and docs not entail searches for specific websites or intent to purchase. Informational search queries can often ultimately lead to online purchases or other calls-to-action, but principally exist at some intermediary point on the buyer journey.

Transactional Queries are made by users who intend to complete a purchase or some other transaction with a business or entity. Such queries often will include action keywords such as "buy", "order", or "contact". Your PPC ads should be focused on these queries, as they are the most likely to deliver decisive action by users. These are where you stand to gain the most ROI for your paid search campaigns.

Keyword Matching Types

In PPC, it is never enough to just enter your target keywords – they must be tailored to their most effective level of search specificity. Many otherwise well-designed paid search campaigns have floundered due to poor keyword matching.

There are two ways to set keyword matching types in Google Ads and other ad platforms. When entering your keywords manually or in bulk, you can use certain punctuation and characters to indicate the type of match. In addition, you can modify keywords already entered in your campaigns by adjusting campaign-level configurations.

Broad Match

Broad match terms are basically the "anything goes" approach to your keywords. Search will broadly match your keyword, including synonyms. If you were using the keyword "hiking boots" with broad match, your ads would trigger even for search terms like "walking boot", "hike show", or "hiking with old boots".

Broad match keywords must be selected sparingly and judiciously. Overuse of broad match can be perilous as it can quickly drain marketing budgets through irrelevant clicks. Google defaults keywords to broad match for a reason – their goal is to maximize clicks, not to maximize your conversions. When manually entering broad match keywords, simply enter them as-is without any special characters or punctuation.

Modified Broad Match

This match type is nearly the same as a standard broad match. The main difference is that you can prevent the algorithm from making substitutions to your keywords. This way, your "hiking boots" keyword might trigger on terms like "boots for hiking" but not a substitution like "shoes for walking". Modified broad matches are manually entered by using a plus sign before each word in your keyword you wish to protect from substitution.

Phrase Match

A phrase match keyword will only trigger on searches that contain the exact phrase as your keywords – unbroken and in the same order. The "hiking boots" ad will thus trigger on searches like "buying hiking boots" but not on "hiking in boots". This is entered manually by enclosing the keyword phrase in parenthesis.

Exact Match

Exact match keywords will only trigger on search terms that match the exact keyword phrase without exceptions or modification. As you might expect, these types of matches often convert more readily than other types, though they tend to be less frequently searched. Exact matches are input by enclosing the keyword phrase in brackets: [ ].

The Anatomy of PPC Ads

Google search ads are constructed by an assemblage of headlines, descriptive text, and a destination URL. You can input as many as fifteen headlines and up to four lines of descriptive text at thirty and ninety characters respectively. When an ad is served, the algorithm assembles the ad from this selection of headlines and descriptions based on what it believes to be relevant to the search query. You do have some limited control over which headlines always appear, but for the most part, the algorithm is in charge.

Google Ads also has a feature called **Ad Extensions**. These are expanded snippets of content that appear below ads that provide additional information about your business. There are several types of extensions you can create, including sitelinks, phone numbers, location info, promotional offers, or even contact forms. Google will also generate extensions automatically if the algorithm see fit to do so.

Creating Effective Ad Copy

An effective PPC campaign relies on the right ad copy. The content of your copy helps determine whether an ad will appear on a search query or not. This means that when crafting the words for your search ad, you have two audiences: the user and the algorithm. In this respect, the mark of an effective search marketer is their ability to accommodate both.

Enticing and Rebuffing Clicks

The role of ad copy in determining whether it will display takes us back to Googles' Quality Score algorithm (see Chapter 10). Part of this algorithm evaluates the copy of your ad for keyword relevance and readability. More relevant ad copy gets assigned a higher quality score and thus a boost in its probability of being served on a search results page. Unfortunately, Google gauges quality strictly on how likely it is to generate clicks rather than generate conversions. Quality Score works for Google, not for you. If you want to succeed with PPC ads, you will need to write ads that are optimized for conversions, and will thus have to go against the strict mores of Quality Score. To this end, you may find that a middling (but not rock-bottom) Quality Score will be where you will have the most success.

PPC ads that work for your interests are those that maximize conversions. This means that it simultaneously must attract and dissuade clicks, depending on the audience. Since you are paying for clicks, you want to entice only potential customers to click on your ads. You also want to do all you can to prevent unlikely customers from clicking – going against the financial interests of Google. Going too far in this direction will hinder the chances of your ads displaying at all. Hence, successful ad copy must strike the balance between these two opposing factors.

Build Around Core Keywords

Every ad group in your campaigns should be based around a single core keyword and its variations. Recall that your PPC keyword list should be centered around transactional search queries. These ads will be shown to users who are likely ready to convert, and so they must be laser-focused on exploiting this mentality. Additionally, focusing your ad groups in such a way will make it much easier to determine which keywords are the most effective (or ineffective) for your PPC strategy. More specificity and focus mean better data.

Focus on Calls to Action

Again, by targeting transactional keyword terms, you will be reaching an audience that is ready to act. Your ad copy, especially the headlines, must grab their attention and lead them toward your call to action.

Flaunt Your Uniqueness

Chances are, you are not an innovator or disruptor in your industry, and neither are most of your competitors. Even so, your business probably has some unique strengths that help you stand out. Identify your best differentiators that make you unique and reflect this in your ad copy

Emotional Triggers

Never forget that your ad copy is being created for people to see and react to. They have hopes, fears, likes, and dislikes. People also tend to be self-centered, especially when engrossed on their phone or computer screens. Your copy should play to these emotional triggers: Personalize the message. Play to the things they love. Speak to the things they dislike.

Psychologically, few things get action more than FOMO – the Fear of Losing Out. It plays to our sense of loss aversion. FOMO is about immediacy: "Act Now!" "Don't Miss Out!" "Limited Time Only!" Urgency is one of the oldest marketing techniques in the book, and still works in online ads. Be sure to utilize measured restraint when employing psychological tactics – this is an ethical consideration.

The Bidding Game

Google Ads, as most of the PPC ad industry it dominates, is based on an auction model. Advertisers place bids against one another to have their ads appear on search results pages or as embedded placements on the display network. They are competing not only for whether their ad will display, but in its relative position on the page. Generally, the highest bidder will win the highest position, with runners-up taking subsequent positions. However, no money is exchanged unless the search user actually clicks on an ad. When this happens, the click is registered, and the advertiser pays Google the amount they bid in the auction.

It bears mentioning that the auction process is not quite as simple as described above. While your maximum bid is a factor in ad placement and ranking, it is not the whole picture. Google uses yet another cleverly named gimmick in these calculations. It's called **Ad Rank**, which takes you and your competitors' ad Quality Score and factors it against your maximum bid amount. From here, your actual cost-per-click is calculated. The way in which this is calculated is more complicated than you might expect, but things are seldom straightforward with Google algorithms.

Bidding Strategies

Google Ad campaigns offer a selection of different bidding strategies that determine the initial configuration of how your keyword bids are structured. A **Bidding Strategy** is a plan for how PPC keyword bids are structured to achieve a goal. Marketing campaigns of all types should be based around specific goals and strategies, and PPC is no different. Your bidding strategy should be tailored to achieve these goals.

You are not required to use Googles' prefab bid strategies. You can start out by using their automated bid recommendations and tweak them manually from there. You can set broad adjustments to every bid within a campaign or even configure them individually. Even if you do not use these settings, you should be aware of what these preset bidding strategies focus on. The goals you have for your PPC campaign will be congruous with at least one of them.

Google bid strategies are principally built around achieving specific targets and/or maximizing certain outcomes within the budget constraints of the campaign. These target outcomes include clicks, conversions, and ad impressions. Bid strategies can also be set to target distinct returns on investment, conversion values, or revenue per click. Some of these strategies, particularly those that involve conversion data, require connecting your website backend to the advertising platform.. For instance, you cannot target specific conversion rates or revenue unless you connect Google Ads to the backend of an E-Commerce platform.

Your Paid Search Goals

Every paid search ad campaign should be built around a specific objective. These will typically encompass a specific call to action: sales orders, sales leads, newsletter signups, etc. These objectives should have measurable goals attached to them, such as a specific volume of sales, leads, or engagements. Google Ads uses a hierarchical structure. Within your campaigns are your ad groups – each of which is specifically targeting one core keywords and its related derivatives. These core keywords represent different subsets of your target audiences. Finally, your individual ads should comprise the direct messaging you utilize in reaching your targeted audience.

As Googles' presets suggest, a **bidding strategy** for meeting campaign goals is often a matter of minimizing or maximizing certain metrics. If your goal is to maximize conversions, then your bidding strategies must focus on increased bidding on the highest converting keywords. Conversely, to maximize conversion value might entail focus more on low-bid keywords. As can be gleamed here, it is called bidding strategy for a purpose – once you have your keywords and ads in order, it all comes down to how you prioritize your bids.

PPC Campaigns and Businesses Development

Any successful marketing strategy entails a process of constant evaluation and improvement, and PPC campaigns are no different. Every aspect of your operation must be periodically inspected and reevaluated. This includes things as specific as your individual ads all the way to your overall marketing goals. As businesses evolve, their marketing needs change and so your paid search objectives will need to accommodate. For instance, for new businesses, customer acquisition is the main priority. As the business becomes more established, priorities shift to customer retention. Organizations that pay attention to their own evolution and react accordingly are far more likely to thrive than those that languish in a static state.

In the context of paid search, you need to ensure your campaigns are evolving along with your business. Recall that your campaigns should all focus on a specific objective. As your business matures, you may need to create new campaigns to accommodate new objectives and/or cancel campaigns that focus on outdated goals. Avoid shifting objectives for existing campaigns – it is far more effective to create new campaigns for new objectives than it is to repurpose an existing one.

The Importance of Data

The Google Ads platform provides an extensive suite of performance analytics. Google provides an extensive array of prefab reports, which can be heavily customized. You can also create custom reports to match your specific information needs. It is important to connect and unify as much of your performance data as you can to maximize your data intelligence. Google Ads can connect to the Google Analytics platform to integrate your website traffic data with your paid search metrics.

If you have an e-commerce website, it is essential that you implement e-commerce tracking in Google Analytics. From this integration, you can connect your online ordering performance data to your paid search data in Google Ads. This data connection is indispensable for e-commerce campaigns, as it enables metrics for tracking ad sales conversions. It also enables reporting on important metrics like return on ad spend (ROAS) and return on investment (ROI).

A common mistake amongst business leaders and marketers is misunderstanding how data tells a story. More data means more accuracy on what is really going on. Search campaigns need to run for a significant amount of time before you have enough information to make a realistic assessment of how they are performing. Time and again, you will see business managers make sweeping changes to otherwise successful marketing campaigns based on a single "off" day or week. These reactionary changes end up diminishing the success of a campaign that, when looked at over a longer period, was performing well. "Off" days and even weeks will happen over any significant period of time, but do not necessarily indicate overall trends. This is a common logical fallacy known as "proof by anomaly". Don't fall for it.

PPC Ads and Natural Selection

Once your keyword and bidding strategies are in order, your ad copy should become the primary focus of your scrutiny. These ads influence both your potential customers as well as your CPCs via the Quality Score. You should be closely monitoring your ad performance reports to see what is and is not working.

It helps to approach your ads with the mindset of natural selection: only the ads that are the most "fit" will survive. You should make regular assessments of your ads – at bimonthly intervals at the very least. This is why you should be dedicating only one keyword per ad group. It creates a well-organized ad structure that enables you to make these evaluations on a keyword-by-keyword basis. This way, you can compare ad performance to one another within an ad group within the same context - they are all serving the same keyword targets.

Returning to the natural selection analogy, your ad groups are akin to a common ecosystem where your ads are organisms competing within it. You should have at least three to five separate ads running in each ad group. These ads reflect the biodiversity of this imaginary ecosystem, as it were. Ads that perform poorly should be rewritten or deleted – evolution or extinction, respectively. Ads that perform well can be left untouched or lightly tweaked.

If you have ads that perform unusually well, you might consider moving them into their own ad groups. Returning one last time to the natural selection analogue, this step is akin to speciation. The benefit of moving high performers to their own groups is that it lets you adjust specific bid amounts for them. It also allows you to create a new ecosystem of ads based on these high performing ads to further evolve them into even better performers.

"It is possible to commit no mistakes and still lose. That is not a weakness; that is life." – Jean-Luc Picard, from Star Trek

---

PART IV: The Internet

Chapter 12: The Internet at Large

No website exists in a vacuum. Beyond the walls of your website is the vastness of the internet. Your audience and potential customers live out there amongst a huge assortment of other websites. Reaching them via search engines, though fundamental, is only the first step toward reaching them. If you wish to thrive online, you must expand your presence beyond your own website to the internet at large.

Your website is the place where you have complete agency over content. You can utilize the search engines indirectly through SEO or directly by paid ads to direct traffic to your site. For SEO, you control the content that search engines consider for indexing. With paid search, you are the one writing your ad listings and how much you are willing to pay for exposure.

Categorizing the Internet

The internet comprises many different types of media. Blogs, social media, forums, news outlets, info portals, videos, and many more promulgate the web. New permutations are always emerging as the internet evolves. Running along the backbone of this assorted content are the search engines in their endless process indexing it all.

Making sense of the assorted types of websites out there starts by categorizing them. In recent years, marketers have adopted the **PESO** model for this purpose. PESO was adapted from the PR (public relations) industry and stands for *paid, earned, shared,* and *owned.*

From a marketing standpoint, PESO has proven to be very useful for categorizing different aspects of the internet landscape. It is comprehensive and covers nearly every permutation of online content. Every PESO category represents a component of the internet that requires specific strategies to utilize in a marketing context. Most importantly, PESO categories clearly describe the extent and type of control you have over the content. This level of control dictates how you should go about optimizing your presence within each.

Paid Media

Paid media comprises every advertising promotion that you pay for. This principally includes paid search and every ad network on the internet. It also can include promoted social media content, native web advertising, app ads, sponsorships, and influencers. Any media that is created or served in exchange for money, goods, or services is paid media.

Earned Media

Earned media emerges when external sources, outlets, or influencers take notice of your business or product and promote it themselves. This type of media is created, owned, and controlled by people completely external to your organization – they are talking about you on their own accord. Paid or "bribed" articles or posts promoting your business are <u>not</u> earned media. Earned media is always free. By virtue of being unpaid, it is generally trusted more by the public. Earned media is not necessarily positive, either. Every person or outlet that can potentially say nice things about you can just as easily go negative. The level of trust earned media has with audiences means negative commentary around your brand can be devastating.

Shared Media

Shared media is primarily comprised of social media, and the terms are often used interchangeably. Principally, shared media is content that users share to their online social circles. Shared media can start from a "seed" of earned or even owned media. For instance, if someone writes a positive article about you on their Facebook, it is earned media. As this post is liked, promoted, shared, or commented on Facebook, it becomes shared media. Another example is an article you post on your own

website that can be shared by site visitors to their social media –
your owned media becomes shared media in this process.

Owned Media

The content that is under your direct control is owned
media. The most conspicuous of this is your website. It can also
include blogs, emails, and apps. Owned media can also apply to
user-generated content that is submitted on your website, such as
reviews and comments (ensure your site TOS is clear to visitors
that their submissions are owned by you).

Hybrids

As with shared content, some types of media might share
characteristics across PESO categories. For instance, you can
create your own company social media pages and accounts. This
content is technically owned media, though the social platforms'
terms of use (TOS) might say otherwise, or at least diminish your
level of control over it.

The Interplay of Content

Though marketers may care about categorizing types of
internet media, the general web audience does not – they simply
go wherever compelling content takes them. Recall back to the
concepts of buyer journeys and marketing funnels. The paths

potential customers might take to ultimately convert into paying customers can cross multiple types of media. A customer could initially learn about your company from a shared social media post, subsequently read an article about you on a review blog, and ultimately find their way to your website. This journey took them from shared, to earned, and ultimately to owned media. Such journeys are the norm, not the exception.

A comprehensive marketing program is incomplete unless its strategy is built on employing multiple permutations of media. If you are not addressing the specific nuances of each type of content, you are fostering breaks in your customer journeys. A customer journey is much like a real-life journey: if the path is incomplete or unclear, the journey to the destination becomes difficult or impossible.

Businesses do not need to focus on every type of PESO media equally. Different businesses and industries require different balances of paid, earned, shared, or owned media. Furthermore, every organization has limited resources, and every type of media cost time and money. These factors necessitate making informed decisions on where to direct your resources.

As every business is different in terms of circumstances and competencies, there is no uniform way to determine your optimal PESO investment. I generally approach this problem by first evaluating where a Business currently lies in its lifecycle and the level of exposure they have with each type of media. If you are just starting out, you may want to focus on owned and paid media. Earned and shared media is more likely to flourish after a business has established itself and has created enough owned content to leverage at scale. If you are overhauling an extant business, your first order of business should be to do a deep audit of where your content gaps are.

Maximizing Your Owned Media

Your most valuable and long-lasting content is likely to be owned media. The principal reason has to do with control – it is utterly yours to do with as you please. Owned media can be created and published as often as you like without having to worry about platform restrictions, rules, or licensing. By contrast, content you post to social media or external sites (guest posts, etc.) are subject to the whims of the platform holders or web administrators. Reliance on such accommodation for your content denies you control and can result in disaster should they decide to delete, alter, or restrict your hard work.

It takes time and money to produce good content, even when you are the sole producer and distributor. In fact, the value of owned media is such that you should devote more care in its development than you would elsewhere. Content you produce for your own website(s) should represent the deepest and highest quality you can muster.

Website and SEO Content

Back in Part III, we discussed in-depth the nature of what your website content should entail. The content you produce on your website should be crafted to serve the interests of your target audiences while being optimized for search indexes.

Blogs

Though not as pervasive as they once were, blogs are still an excellent venue to build up your owned media. If anything, they create a perfect "excuse" to produce regular articles and other media. This is a good option for making content that might not necessarily fit into the navigational structure of your website. For example, articles reflecting timely or seasonal information are a better fit for a blog update than a static page on your main site.

Satellite websites

This is a gray area and might fly too close to black hat SEO but is worth mentioning. A satellite website is a secondary site on a separate domain that provides industry or niche-relevant content and links to your main website. One example would be an instructional or tutorial website providing advice on how to manage drywall repairs. On the surface, this website provides relevant information to visitors looking for information on how to repair a wall. However, the actual purpose is to ultimately send visitors (and search crawlers) to your business website that sells your line of drywall repair kits.

Some marketers justify this approach because these sites provide useful free information to visitors who might be repelled by a site with a commercial agenda. Some SEOs employ this tactic as a means of creating additional backlinks to their main websites. The ethical problems here are clear, but this approach has proven effective for some businesses. If you feel you need to do this, then be transparent about it and indicate clearly that the site provides helpful free information - courtesy of your brand.

Micro Websites

Like satellite websites, a micro website is a separate site with a singular branding purpose. The distinction with a micro site is that it is unambiguously an extension of your business. The best use of a micro site is for promoting a specific part of your business like a single product or service. Such sites employ content such as videos and presentations that are laser-focused on the narrow topic of the site. An example would be a new blend of whiskey with a distinctive name, design, and branding. This product is special and having a small website dedicated to its uniqueness can help propel its launch.

Some micro websites utilize their own dedicated domain name. This is useful in the case of a trademarked product or service that leans heavily on its branding. Domain names are a big part of online branding, and so a micro website is an ideal way to capitalize on this. However, from an SEO perspective, you run the risk of limiting your reach by splitting your pagerank across multiple sites. Considering this, you might want to instead consider utilizing a subdomain for your micro site.

Emails

Do not forget that emails are also owned media. These days, there is no excuse for a business not to employ email marketing campaigns. Generating email marketing lists via signup forms on your website is easier than ever. However, you are obligated to provide useful or interesting content in your messages. Why would anyone give you their email address if they were not getting something good in return? Email-exclusive content and generous price promotions further the incentive.

Though the content of your emails is owned by you, be sure to stay on the good side of email practices. Obey all spam guidelines and provide easy ways to unsubscribe. Nearly all bulk email providers require these best practices in their terms of use.

The consequences of spamming emails can be severe where – entailing cancellation by email marketing providers or even having your domain blocked by ISPs.

Owned Media and the External Internet

Your owned media should create "hooks" that attract peoples' attention. This in turn can entice people to talk about it and share on social media. External blogs, news sites, and aggregators are in the business of finding and creating new content for their readers. The more quality content you have, the more likely you are to have posts and articles written about you. A large amount of owned media also creates a sense of authority that can make it much easier for you to reach out to these external sites to see if they are interested. This process is discussed further in Chapter 14.

"Opportunities multiply as they are seized." – Sun Tzu

Chapter 13: Paying Your Way

Though pay-per-click search advertising is the dominant avenue of paid online marketing, it does not comprise the entirety of that space. There are many other advertising networks that are happy to take your marketing dollars. Once you have your search marketing strategy locked-in, you should consider the assortment of alternative online marketing options. For the scope of this chapter, we will not be discussing paid advertising offered on social media platforms – that will be covered in-depth in Chapter 17.

The Google Display Network

The **Google Display Network** (GDN) is part of the Google Ads platform. It contrasts with Googles' search network in a very consequential way: Ads do not appear as part of search results but instead appear on blogs, videos, Gmail, forums, apps, content aggregators, and more. These ads display as embedded elements or overlays on webpages. When you click on one of these ads, the owner of the website on which it was shown gets a cut of your per-click bid.

Running ads on the GDN is simple, as it is merely a campaign-level setting in Google Ads. You can even run a campaign on both networks at once. This is not advisable, as the differences between them are stark enough that a single campaign strategy cannot effectively accommodate both. Always run your search and display campaigns separately. In addition, you should not consider placing ads on the GDN until your regular search campaigns are in good shape.

The major drawback to this type of advertising is that the ads are shown to audiences who are in "browse" mode rather than active search. Recall the two types of search queries: **Informational queries**, where they are seeking specific information on a problem or interest; and **transactional queries**, made by users who intend to make a purchase or other such action. In both cases, the audience on the search network are interested in specific information and are more likely to commit to your calls-to-action. On the display network, the audience is browsing, not searching. Users are engaged with the content of the webpages themselves - not the ads served there.

Simply put, the difference between search and display advertising comes down to user intention. To attract clicks with a display ad, you are competing with the webpage for the users' attention. Nobody goes to a blog or watches a video because they want to see the commercials. This simple fact makes the audience on display networks far less responsive than those who are actively searching for specific information. They are in a completely different mode of intent and are far less likely to commit to your calls-to-action even if they do click.

Another problem with display networks in general is they appear on many low-quality websites. Integrating display ads on a webpage is relatively simple from a technical standpoint. The display network has an economic incentive to make it as easy as possible to place ads on sites. Thus, the internet is flooded with tons of poor-quality sites that exist only to push clicks on their embedded ads by way of sheer volume. In addition, there are many unethical websites that are setup to generate clicks through misleading and fraudulent means.

Though not nearly as effective as search marketing, the GDN does have some benefits. One of the best uses of the display network is for branding and mindshare development. Building brand recognition for a business or product requires repetition. The more a person sees branded messaging online, the more it "sticks" with them – even if only subconsciously. Furthermore, display ads are good at reaching narrow audiences. Even the most obscure interests have an online presence on blogs, forums, and other websites to serve the niche. You can target these sites to get your branding in front of these audiences.

It would be remiss not to mention **remarketing**, the practice of "following" a user around the internet and show them ads based on their search and browsing behavior. A person who has searched for drywall repair information or visited drywall repair websites is flagged as being interested in…drywall repair. They are then subsequently shown ads on other websites they visit – even sites that have nothing to do with drywall. Such ads will show up wherever they encounter the display network.

The advantage to remarketing is clear in that it pushes ads to users with an established interest your product or brand. However, privacy concerns have become a very hot topic in recent years. People have become increasingly wary of having their online life tracked, and few things throw this in their face as blatantly as remarketed ads (pun intended). This makes many people understandably upset and can be a liability to your online reputation. I saw this first-hand in my professional life in e-commerce: We would get frequent complaints from customers about us "stalking" them online with our ads. Angering customers is not how you want to run your business, and so you must take this into careful consideration.

The tide seems to be turning against remarketing as we know it. Privacy concerns are beginning to dominate the online zeitgeist. Google itself intends to seriously stymie remarketing with their moves to "kill" 3rd party cookies. Other advertising services are also moving to revise or even eliminate remarketing in their suites. Time will tell just how "dead" remarketing is, but its future is not as bright as it once was.

Other Advertising Networks

The Google Display Network is only one of many similar types of display ad networks. These competitors offer advertising under the same paradigm as the GDN. Examples of these alternative display networks include Taboola and Outbrain. Additionally, as Google has their display network, so do the other major search engines' ad platforms.

The principal difference between these networks and GDN is that they serve different client websites on which to display their ads – some of which can be quite large and influential. Smaller display networks may serve less significant client sites but make up for it in terms of sheer quantity and comparatively lower costs.

When should you consider using an alternative display network? GDN, as it is part of the Google Advertising platform, is by far the largest, and it should be your first choice. Utilize other display networks as supplemental placements. Your main consideration should be which client websites they serve and if your target audiences are on there. Most advertisement services provide information and stats on their audiences and reach. Never use an ad platform that cannot provide this basic information!

The wider world of display ads features different types of ad placements. Standard display ads comprise placed content that is unambiguously an advertisement. These lie in specified locations on the page and are most commonly image-based ads.

Pop-up ads are just that: ads that overlay over the content of the webpage either instantaneously, after a delay, or after the user moves their mouse to certain areas. As disruptive and unpopular as these ad types are, they still exist for a reason – they get results, believe it or not.

Then there are so-called **native ads**. These are placed on the page in such a manner to appear to be part of the core, or native, page content. Native ads can be quite misleading, as people can easily mistake them for "real" site content. Native ads thus generate more clicks, which is good for the ad platform. The peril of these ads is that clicking on them sends users to the ad landing page outside the native site they clicked from. If the user thought they were navigating to another page on the site they were browsing, it can be disruptive to their experience – they ended up somewhere they did not expect or intend to go. Such a situation can leave users feeling mislead and so are far less likely to convert on your landing page, let alone ever come back. Users who feel especially aggrieved are likely to associate your brand in a negative light.

Sponsored Content

Sponsored content is a type of promotional media that an advertiser (the sponsor) has paid a publisher to create and distribute. This content appears on the publishers' website and other distribution outlets. Unlike a traditional advertisement, this content is an actual element of the native website. Basically, you are paying a website to place content on their site to promote your brand or product.

Sponsored content often carries with it a higher level of trust and quality than a typical ad. The best sites that offer sponsored content are in the business of producing content regularly, and so bring with it a level of professional touch. This can be an effective way to promote your business – especially on sites that are themed around your target audience.

There are two important things to look out for with sponsored content. First is the ethical matter of transparency with your audience. Scrupulous content sites will make sure to label sponsored content as such. The second and most pressing issue has to do with ownership. This can often be a murky area from a legal standpoint unless you take proactive measures. As you do not ultimately own the content you are paying to have created and/or distributed, its availability online is subject to the publisher. Tread carefully, read the fine print, and thoroughly review all such agreements before paying for sponsored content.

Affiliate Marketing

Affiliate marketing is one of the older advertising models on the internet. It is when a publisher, such as a blogger, gets a cut of sales generated through their webpage. Affiliate publishers place links or ads on their site in much the same way as a typical display ad. However, where display ad providers get paid whenever a click happens, affiliates only get paid when a clickthrough converts into a sale.

Using affiliate advertisers has several upsides for businesses. You only pay the advertiser when a sale is made, so the financial risk is comparatively low. Since the affiliate is paid based on performance, they have an incentive to place their links in contexts that encourages sales over clicks. Affiliate advertising networks are attractive to content publishers of all sizes, and it is easy for creators to place affiliate links on their sites in hopes of monetizing them. This ease of use and potential for earnings means affiliate networks have a far reach in terms of sheer quantities of participating websites.

Affiliate marketing is far from perfect and has some big drawbacks. Affiliate ads commonly look and behave like standard display ads. Display ads generally have low clickthrough rates, and affiliate links are no different. As affiliates only get paid by conversions rather than clicks, many of them resort to shady means of boosting performance. Additionally, there are a LOT of affiliate-oriented websites. Many of these websites are mass-produced, low-quality sites that are little more than glorified linkfarms.

Utilizing affiliate marketing networks is relatively easy, and they function much like other online advertising providers. While you only pay by conversions, these platforms also include monthly service fees, and they commonly take a cut of the affiliate commission themselves. If you decide to use an affiliate ad provider, you should be looking at three things. The first is to investigate the quality of the affiliate sites they serve. Stay away from providers who predominately serve low-quality spam sites. Next, make sure you clearly understand the fee and compensation structure of the provider. Other than the commission rates and operating fees, you need to know how long the **attribution window** is – the time between a click and a sale where the affiliate can get credit for the conversion.

Shopping Campaigns

You may notice that Google and Bing searches often return product listings in their search results pages. These are their respective shopping ad services in action. Aside from Amazon, search engines are a principal way in which people search, browse, and discover products online. Google and Bing only display shopping ads for searches they deem relevant for them. The best way to determine if your products are a fit for this ad model is to check for your competitors. If you do searches for your specific or similar products and shopping ads come up, then you have a good indication that your shopping ads will display too.

Though their cost model is PPC based, these ad placements differ from standard ads in some important ways. First, they are only relevant for physical products sold online. They also are required to have product images attached. Finally, these ads require a bit more technical work to setup than normal ads - products are populated to shopping ad platforms via data feeds.

Just as with the rest of the search industry, Google Shopping is vastly larger than Bings', and should be the first focus of your shopping strategy. Fortunately, the setup and configuration for Bing shopping ads closely mirrors that of Google. As shopping ads are for physical products only, you must have your own e-commerce website. You will also need to setup a Google Merchant account and connect it to your Google Shopping account. The last part of setup involves your data feed – a list of products and their attributes for Google to populate ads from. This data feed is formatted in XML and requires certain attributes such as name, image URL (where your product image is located), price, product availability, product URL (the exact landing page where the product can be purchased), product SKU or ID, product brand, and price. The biggest pain point in managing shopping ads is maintaining the XML feed – especially if you have many or frequently changing products. Fortunately, many e-commerce platforms now offer automations that generate and synchronize these shopping feeds.

Working With Influencers

The rise of the social internet created an entirely new avenue through which trends and brands take root and spread: the Influencer. **Influencers** are popular personalities and content creators who boast sizable numbers of online followers. These individuals are chiefly valued by their followers for their opinions on specific subjects or themes. Oftentimes, they exhibit interesting or quirky personalities – most often a carefully curated façade. Influencers are named for the trust they garner amongst their followers, and hence the influence they have over them. Influencers can have a great deal of sway over the opinions of their followers, and thus present tremendous value to marketers. To make it as an influencer is to win a popularity contest – they need not be an expert in a subject to be regarded as one by the masses.

Though influencers do promote brands that they genuinely like for free, they make a living by selling access to their audience and messaging.

Influencers can be incredibly useful for promoting a brand and building lasting online clout. Their importance in online marketing has steadily increased in recent years and shows no sign of diminishing anytime soon. The precursors to modern influencers were bloggers. Though blogs still form an important niche in the online landscape, this space is decidedly dominated by social influencers. Part of the power of influencers is that they generally build their online identity around specific topics and interest categories. You can find influencers in virtually every topic or community that exists on the social internet. Additionally, influencers work hard to establish and grow dedicated audiences who are interested in them due to their topical focus. Part of the appeal influencers have with their audiences is trust and spontaneity. Successful influencers present themselves as unscripted and honest personalities who are easy for their audiences to identify with. In an age of marketing cynicism and ad blockers, influencers can cut right through and reach audiences that traditional advertising simply cannot.

Influencer Marketing is the practice of leveraging social influencers as part of an online marketing strategy. Not all influencers are created equal in terms of reach, experience, or expertise, so you may have to weed through many to find a good fit. The influencer industry has matured enough where standard practices and advertiser networks have emerged. As full-fledged businesses, many influencers utilize managers, staff, or agencies to manage their promotional offerings. This reveals both the extent of the influencer industry and the competitive landscape for marketers – the most prominent influencers are thus harder to reach and are more expensive to hire.

The cost of paid influencer campaigns depends on several factors. Prominent influencers generally cost more than smaller ones. Some campaigns are paid based on a cut of performance, such as commissions. Some influencers will accept product discounts or free samples in exchange for coverage. More straightforward compensation is based on costs per social post, video, shout-out, or mention. If you reached your influencer through an agency or service, expect to pay additional commissions or platform fees.

Should you use an influencer, and if so which one? These questions are answered by looking to your target audiences - specifically your marketing personas. If your target audiences can be found amongst influencer audiences, it is a good indication they can be a powerful part of your overall marketing strategy. Influencers primarily operate on social media platforms, and so your research on those will undoubtedly determine if and who they are. There are also platforms known as **Influencer Marketplaces** that exist to connect marketers with influencers. Some of these platforms even handle the legal, logistical, and payments for you. Many PR firms are beginning to specialize in pairing brands with influencers as well. All professional influencers will be able to provide detailed data on their followers – including psychographics, demographics, and location. You should be looking for your marketing personas among the audiences of your potential partner influencers. In addition, as influencers strive to be relatable to their audiences, they should bear similarities to your personas themselves.

When you have identified an influencer who caters to your target audience(s), you must consider their potential efficacy. Just because they have an audience is no guarantee they can create results. First and foremost, any influencer you partner with must be a fit for your brand – their personality must be consistent with your brand identity. For instance, a family-friendly brand is a poor fit for an influencer who has a decidedly adult or crass style, regardless of how large their audience is. It is extremely important to become deeply familiar with the personality and tone of any influencer you consider working with. Audiences will associate your brand with the personality of the influencers who promote it. Ensure there is nothing to their body of work and demeanor that you do not want to rub off on your public perception.

As with every other aspect of marketing, your influencer partnerships must be built around specific objectives. Any influencer you utilize should be able to effectuate the type of audience response you are looking for. It also means that you provide the influencer with the tools they need to achieve these goals as well. For example, if you are running an influencer campaign to generate online sales, you should provide offer discounts, gifts, or promo codes. Remember, influencer marketing is more like a partnership than an advertising buy – you must work together and be on the same page in achieving your marketing objectives.

Finding an influencer who is a good fit for your brand is half the battle. The other half is working with them in crafting the right messaging. Some marketers and business leaders make the mistake of trying to micromanage influencer campaigns. While it is understandable to be wary of limited control over the message, this goes against the strength of influencer marketing. Influencers hold sway over their audiences because they are seen as authentic. The entire purpose of using an influencer is to capitalize on this goodwill. If you did your research and ensured they are a good tonal fit for your brand, then you should trust their judgement and expertise. Obviously, you will have boundaries and requirements for the influencer to follow. However, you must give them enough discretion to be genuine and authentic.

Unlike traditional ad buying, influencer marketing is focused more on relationships. If you see good results with an influencer campaign, you would do well to further cultivate your business relationship with them. Influencer marketing, like most social media, is neither perennial nor evergreen – it is focused on the immediate present. Ongoing influencer campaign relationships are crucial to keeping your brand in the minds of their audiences. Therefore, you should go into every influencer campaign as you would a long-term business relationship.

Influencers are especially crucial in marketing to younger people. They are more likely to be consuming a varied online media diet and are accustomed to influencer culture. In addition, they are less likely to respond to traditional advertising. Millennials and Gen-Z are more likely to discover brands and new ideas through relationships with their online peers than older generations. If your brand is struggling to connect with younger audiences, one of your first steps in overhauling your marketing strategy is partnering with influencers. Influencer marketing is the new normal.

"People don't turn down money. It's what separates us from the animals." – Jerry Seinfeld

---

Chapter 14: Getting Recognized

Website content is created to get noticed, but not all content is created equal. People will pay attention to good content and will likely encourage others to take a look. Websites that offer sparse or poor-quality content will quickly be long forgotten – the best they can do is be supported by paid links until money runs out. The key to the longevity of a website is the extent to which it garners repeated attention and discussion. This discussion is the "buzz" your website fosters. Buzz manifests in many ways including word-of-mouth, social sharing, influencers, and articles.

This spontaneous and free content is the essence of earned media, which first described back in Chapter 12. Earned media is incredibly valuable for online promotion. From a marketing standpoint, earned media is akin to organic search results. It is "free" and regarded as more trustworthy than paid placements. As with SEO, it can happen all on its own but is more likely when you apply time and effort to help it along.

Trust

One of the biggest reasons earned media is so valuable is trust. People trust earned media because it is coverage and opinion provided without a monetary agenda. Of course, this is not true without qualification – people trust earned media from *respected* sources, or at least sources *they* respect. For example, more people will trust information from a well-known reporter than a blogger on a backwater website. Furthermore, a person will likely trust a source that is congruous with their political or social leanings than ones who do not.

Paid advertising will always carry a taint of untrustworthiness. Even the most charismatic influencers or entertaining commercials will not completely surmount this distrust. This is neither unexpected nor a bad thing for society. However, it's not good news for the efficacy of your advertising budget. Advertising spend will always be required, but maximizing your marketing necessitates the facilitation of free, trusted information about your brand.

Beware the temptation to disguise paid media as earned media. As much as people distrust paid advertising, they distrust and despise companies that try to fool them even more. Back in 2006, Sony commissioned an ad company to create a fake blog to promote their PSP gaming hardware. This blog was presented to look like the personal blog of some teenagers who were trying to convince their parents to buy them a PSP for Christmas. Nowhere on the website or any of the content therein had any indication it was a paid marketing campaign. Reporters and internet sleuths quickly discovered that the site was a marketing stunt. Consumers were not happy nor amused with this attempted deception. Sony, after initially denying they had anything to do with it, had a major PR mess to clean up. It would be years before they moved past the anger and distrust they garnered from this stunt. Adding insult to injury, it did not help that the blog itself was insultingly stupid.

Even if you have no intention on disguising any of your paid media, you would do well to ensure you are not appearing to do so. Sponsored content and native ad placements are the closest you should get to blurring the line between paid and earned media – they match the site they are placed in as if they were native content. Should you choose to utilize these, make sure that the placements are clearly labeled as advertising. This is more than an ethical concern, as the negativity from appearing to be deceitful can far undo any benefit.

The Grey Areas of Earned Media

Many marketers and PR experts look to the PESO model as immutable gospel and fail to see it for what it is: incredibly useful, yet imperfect. All classification systems are artificial and imperfect, and that does not diminish their utility.

Marketers sometimes blur this line when it comes to influencers. Influencers are seen as a major part of the earned media landscape. However, influencers do not work for free and expect to be compensated for any traffic or buzz they send your way. If an influencer is getting paid to create content, then it is paid media. SOme marketers regard influencers as being intrinsically in the earned media realm. This is often justified by compensating them with free samples. Sometimes, influencers might take payment in exchange for coverage of your product or service but make no promises as to tone or positivity – a grey area both ethically and categorically if ever there was one!

The distinguishing characteristic of earned media is that it is unpaid third-party content. Its creator and publisher must be completely unrelated to the brand or product it is promoting. Technically, you could regard all content shared or promoted on social media as being earned media. This is a valid observation. However, social media is very distinct in its nature and implementation. Social media will be covered in Part V of this book.

Content is King, Again

Web content must be usable and interesting to visitors; readable by search crawlers; and rich in keywords and metadata to get ranked by search engines. In the context of earned media, it must also be compelling enough to encourage people to promote it on their own. Much like SEO, facilitating earned media can be bolstered by specific tactics. Just as you create webpages to target keywords for search, you do the same for earned engagement.

If you are already in the practicing of creating interesting new content for your visitors, then what is so different with content targeting earned media? Most good content has the potential to get external attention and promotion. However, people are more likely to discuss things that encourage self-reflection. In addition, little known facts about compelling topics get people to pay attention – discovering the extraordinary in the ordinary resonates with everyone. Another way to get people talking about your content is through controversy. Shock-tactics may have had their efficacy in the past but is inadvisable today. Internet rage is faster and more intense than ever and is almost never worth the hassle. Stay positive as much as possible.

You can never predict when or if any of your website content will resonate enough to generate earned media. However, you should ensure that your site makes it as easy as possible for it to happen. Every content page on your site should have technological hooks to ensure it is as easy to share or reference. These hooks can include share buttons for social media and click-to-email features. If you have video or audio content, provide the ability for visitors to easily embed it elsewhere on the internet. This is commonly done through providing embedding code below the media – most audio and video creation software allows for you to generate these.

The Power of Media Kits

Many websites are unprepared for success with earned media, and it can cost them opportunities for exposure. Just as general internet audiences have low tolerance when it comes to locating information, so do bloggers, journalists, and other earned influencers. To this end, your business must maintain media kits. These are the key to providing quick and clear company information for interested parties.

A **media kit** is an easy-to-understand batch of general information regarding a person, business, or organization. Media kits are intended to provide the reader with a full overview and understanding about you. In general, a media kit should provide insights into your brands' background, story, and place in your industry. It must represent your "best foot forward" and focus on accolades, accomplishments, milestones, and flattering statistics. For organizations, media kits need to contain an overview of its operational principals and identify who is in charge of media relations.

Press kits are often used interchangeably with media kits. Though similar in nature, they have different objectives. Press kits are more topical in focus than media kits. Media kits are principally evergreen and describe your organization in general terms. Press kits revolve around specific events, products, or initiatives. They are called press kits because they are primarily provided to journalists writing a story on a specific topic and need a quick and reliable fact sheet for reference.

Your media and press kits must be easy to locate and obtain. It is best to have them in a singular, "portable" file format such as a PDF, so it is easy to email and download. If you have the resources, you can create full webpage versions as well – they make for effective SEO pages. Links to your media kits must be super-easy to locate on your website – typically placed in your footer.

Getting the Word Out

Generating earned coverage is more proactive than just making your content and hoping it gets noticed on its own. You need to get the word out and help it get as much exposure as you can. More exposure means more opportunities for it to find interest on the internet at large.

The first thing you must do for your content is synergize it across every channel under your control. Integrate your content into every part of your operation. When you deploy new content or products to your site, post a summary and link on all your social media channels. If you utilize email newsletters, promote content posts with either their own dedicated email campaign or as part of your recurring newsletter campaigns. Depending on the layout of your website, you can promote new or relevant content on all your pages. This can be done via links in your headers and footers or even popups where appropriate. Maximize the exposure of your content by making the most of the audiences you are already reaching across all your channels.

Though not nearly as important as they once were, press releases are still useful methods to get attention. Press releases must be about valid topics of note like announcements of mergers, acquisitions, partnerships, or new product rollouts. They must be relevant and used sparingly – don't be like the boy who cried "wolf" and end up having your releases ignored when something truly remarkable comes up. Distribution of press releases starts with the same infrastructure you use to promote any new content you create – blog posts, social media, newsletters, etc. Furthermore, links to your releases should be compiled in the same areas of your site that host your media and press kits. There are also numerous mass outlets to submit your press releases to in hopes of it getting picked up by journalists or publishers. Examples include the venerable Newswire and PRnewswire.

Targeting Outlets

Just as you have target customer personas, so too should you maintain a list of media outlets you would like to target for coverage. Be realistic in making this list and remember to focus on outlets who reach your desired audiences. Chances are your business is unlikely to be of interest to BBC headline news but would be for an industry or niche-specific outlet.

Do not limit your targets to only "traditional" websites that publish articles, either. Video and audio podcasts, once fringe, are now the hottest outlets for earned media coverage out there. Best of all, podcasts and web video shows are often focused on very specific topics. You can find shows that target nearly every niche and audience out there – there are likely many who serve your target audiences.

Once you have your full list of target websites, podcasts, writers, and other creators, you must get on their radar screens. The most straightforward way to start a relationship is with a simple "hello". However, there are rules to the game and the people behind these outlets are very busy and inundated with requests. You need to stand out, make a good impression, and not commit any potentially damaging breaks in protocol. Err on the side of being professional than creative or cute. This begins with research about the outlets and the people behind them. Make sure you are contacting the right people and not just cold contacting any email address you find.

If you are running all or part of a business online, then you have some expertise in your field and industry. You can leverage this expertise to get yourself and your business exposure. Journalists, bloggers, and content writers are always in need of expert sources for information, research, and topics. Hence, you would do well to network with such individuals. Professional networks like LinkedIn are a common place to people to connect and proclaim their expertise. In addition, outlets such as HARO (Help A Reporter Out) exist to connect journalists and writers with topical experts. If you are not leveraging your own personal expertise and skillset, you are passing up many opportunities for exposure.

Finessing Negative Content

One of the drawbacks of earned media is your lack of control over it. You only control what you own and what you paid for. Inevitably, any business that has been online long enough will experience negative earned media – even if you feel you didn't really "earn" it. Though it has always been a part of business, the speed and scope at which the internet works can amplify even small issues.

You cannot control the certitude of negative media, but you can control how you respond to it. Do not wait for it to happen first – get a plan in place ASAP. Planning helps you respond with certainty and clarity. It also helps counteract the high emotions you might feel during a negative attack. A poor, heated, disorganized, or non-response to negativity can make the situation infinitely worse.

Do Not Ignore

It never helps to ignore negative press or comments. Even if the "offence" might be trivial or unreasonable to you, most of the public will likely not see it that way. Ignoring will look like you either do not care or are guilty of whatever the issue is.

Consult Legal Counsel

Before you take any action responding to negative media, consult with your legal counsel. There can be some serious long-lasting liability issues at play. For instance, apologizing for something can be seen as an admission of liability. The internet remembers everything, so play it safe.

Acknowledge and Correct

Recognize the issue at hand and do not argue. If there is any incorrect information being circulated, you must correct it.

This must be done with care and restraint. Present facts and corrections in a measured manner and never appear hostile with "gotchas". Do not appear defensive or angry.

Apologize

If you are responsible for what caused the negativity, then apologize immediately. In fact, for most minor matters, apologies can diffuse much of the issue outright – even if you truly are not at fault.

Provide Positives, but do so Sparingly

Unless you are incompetent or a swindler, you probably have some good customer feedback or other examples of your good reputation. Sprinkle in some of these in your responses to negativity. Take care not to lean too heavily into this tactic and go overboard. Too much can appear desperate or even passive aggressive.

Utilize Owned and Social Media

The venues to which you respond to negative media should be under your control. Though social media responses present some peril due to the presence of user comments, it is still your best way to immediately communicate to your audience. However, your principal location for any official missives should be your own website. Link from social media to your response page.

Equip Employees

If you have customer-facing employees at any level, you owe it to them and your business reputation to provide them with official responses to any known negative media. It helps you control the messaging across your organization and makes things easier for your personnel. Consistency of messaging is critical, and your personnel must all be on the same page.

Consult a PR Firm

Sometimes, managing negativity can turn out to be an overwhelming affair – especially for a small business. If you are facing a particularly far-reaching instance of negative press, you might do best to bring in experts. There is an entire branch of the PR (public relations) industry that specializes in this very type of issue.

"Trust takes years to build, and seconds to destroy" – unknown

---

PART V: Social Media

Chapter 15: Leveraging Social Media

Though online communities existed since the earliest days of the internet, the advent of broadband and smartphones changed everything. Faster internet made sharing photos and video easy. Smartphones and their built-in cameras enabled people to share virtually every moment of their lives instantly. Where social media was once a novelty, it is now an integral part of our daily lives. For better or worse.

Today, social media is so omnipresent that it is a necessity for online businesses to leverage it. If your business does not have a social media presence, it may as well not exist at all. This is true even for businesses that have little to do or say on social media. It is so ubiquitous that potential customers often see lack of a social presence as a red flag. Such businesses need not maintain a full-featured social media footprint, but they need to have a Facebook page at the very least. Social media creates social proof and indicates to many people whether a business is "real" or not.

Social Media Algorithms

On social media, businesses must contend with the realities of how their algorithms curate content. As one might expect, social media algorithms are laser-focused on monetization. There are three ways people will find you on social media: direct access, paid placement, and suggestions from the algorithm. Direct access is just that – people follow an external link directly to your social landing page. Paid placements work much like other ad networks and will be discussed later. Finally, there is whatever the algorithm decides to place in users' feeds. The **feed** is the list of auto-curated content presented on a social media platform.

Social feeds are algorithmically designed to present content to users based on relevancy to their interests. Typically, you will not see every post from every person or organization you follow on a social platform. The algorithm decides what posts you see and in what order they come in. While the "newness" of the content is a factor, the system prioritizes topical relevancy. Relevant to what? Social platforms utilize extensive data collection and powerful AI to create detailed psychological profiles of users. The power of this AI cannot be understated – they can extrapolate an immense amount of information about you with terrifying accuracy. Depending on the extent of your usage, they can determine your interests, habits, mindset, and what is going in in your life. The extent of this psychographic information wielded by social platforms is precisely why there is an increasing public ambivalence toward social media and big data.

Social feeds do more than show you content from people and organizations you follow. It leverages the information it knows about you to provide recommendations for new content that might be of interest. This is part of the power of social media for businesses – the power of discovery. So far, the concessions social platforms have made to privacy concerns have not diminished this power. Regardless of what the future holds for social media and privacy, it will always be an imperative for your business to leverage it.

Be In the Right Places

Many businesses are tempted to get onto every social media platform they can. This can be an expensive endeavor, as creating social content isn't free and managing social accounts is time-consuming. Also, social media platforms are created equal – they all have different media presentation paradigms with contrasting audiences, capacities, and investment. Regardless, the one platform you should be on no matter what is Facebook. As the "Google of social media", it is so large and ubiquitous that it cannot be ignored. Choosing additional social platforms is contingent on your business's audiences and brand identity.

You need to be on the social media networks that are most relevant to your brand and where your target customers are likely to reside. This comes down to the research you have on your target audiences. This will entail utilizing your customer personas, as covered back in Chapter 6. The next step is to research the various social platforms to see which ones cater to your target audiences. Nearly every social platform provides such data, especially as part of their respective paid advertising suites. For instance, Facebook has a feature called *Audience Insights* that outlines stats on target audiences on the platform. Other platforms provide similar metrics.

Never ignore your competitors when researching social media. Determine which social platforms your competitors are on and the respective scope and size of their presence there. Many social outlets provide metrics upfront about the popularity of businesses and trends. For instance, Facebook will show you how many likes and followers a business has right on their front page. There are also numerous paid research tools out there that can do detailed analysis of competitors and their social reach. They can be expensive, but the data they generate can be of immense value.

Meet the Social Media Platforms

Books such as this are impossible to future-proof and are outdated soon after publishing. Listing players in social media and their characteristics is one such way of dating this book. Nonetheless, the following is a list of the biggest players in social media as of writing. This list is far from comprehensive or representative of the comparative sizes of each entity. Pay attention to the differences in approaches these platforms take in delivering their social media experience. The takeaway should be that there are many different social paradigms online – the only way to compete and thrive in the social media industry is this uniqueness.

Facebook AKA Meta

Facebook is the juggernaut in social media. They began a rebranding of the company in 2021, now calling themselves Meta. They boast a massive user base of billions of individuals. Millions of businesses use Facebook pages for their principal social media presence. Facebook is easy to use because it supports nearly every type of content format: text, images, videos, and livestreams. The platform is also known for its notorious content curation algorithm, which has been blamed for contributing to the epidemics of mental illness, misinformation, and political extremism. Such is an example of the immense, perhaps unprecedented power that Facebook has in modern society.

Twitter

Twitter emphasizes current real-time information in a short form posting style - it allows for only 280 characters per post. Hashtags are prevalent on Twitter and is the main way in which topics are compartmentalized. The real-time focus of Twitter makes it popular for current news across nearly topical interest imaginable. This is a great platform for businesses to post timely updates and info releases to the public.

Reddit

The "front page of the internet", Reddit is an online forum that caters to nearly every topic imaginable. Users can upload links, images, and videos. Discussions, divided into "subreddits" can be responded and referenced in a threaded layout. There are subreddit communities that cover an immense array of topics and interests, making it invaluable for targeting niche audiences. Reddit can be thought of as the largest discussion board on the internet.

TikTok

A short-form video sharing social network, TikTok is known for its reach with younger people. Videos, which can be up to sixty seconds in length, can be recorded and edited right in its app and posted immediately. The bite-sized videos mean users can quickly see content from multiple sources in short periods. TikTok is very influencer-oriented and is often the point of origin for many trends in online culture.

YouTube

Owned by Google, YouTube is second only to Facebook in terms of active users. YouTube has a vast trove of amateur and professionally created video content spanning countless subjects. Many people do not think of YouTube as a social media platform, but as primarily a video site. However, it harbors a vast community maintained by viewer comments and responses. Since anyone can create and upload videos instantly, YouTube has a huge community of vloggers (video bloggers) and influencers.

The connection to Google is the biggest part of the influence of YouTube. Video content is more popular than ever, and the emergence of 5G wireless will only make it even more so. YouTube is also powered by Google search. This makes YouTube video content a significant venue for businesses and brands to be found via search and discovery. In addition, the Google Display Network (GDN) serves ads to YouTube, which is one of its comparative business advantages.

LinkedIn

What was once a job posting site has evolved into the dominant social media site for professionals. It is a place where experts connect and network with others in their respective industries. Aside from talent acquisition, businesses utilize

LinkedIn to establish their industry expertise and authority. LinkedIn can bring social proof to your business and is also a must if you are competing for good talent to hire. Most knowledge workers look to LinkedIn business presences to evaluate them for job considerations.

In terms of marketing, LinkedIn is a better fit for B2B (business to business) than general consumer sales (B2C). The social context of the platform is work-related, so users there are far less interested in personal transactions than they are business purchasing. This is what makes the audiences on LinkedIn so valuable as they are categorized by professional interests and roles.

Snapchat

Snapchat is based on sharing photos, chats, and short-form videos among groups of friends. The principal gimmick of Snapchat is its temporary format - content is deleted automatically after a short time (users can still save some content manually). Snapchat is also notable for popularizing the "stories" format. A **story** is an automatically refreshing sequence of status messages interspersed arranged around a common a narrative or theme. Stories are now an important part of many other social platforms.

For businesses, the biggest holdup here is that the content you create is not evergreen, and some managers are not comfortable with that. Fortunately, Snapchat has a complete display ads platform if you do not have the stomach to see your content disappear.

Instagram

Instagram is a very popular platform for sharing various types of visual content including videos, photos, and livestreams. Marketers like Instagram because its audience has a comparatively high level of interaction with brands. Instagram offers an array of tools for businesses to leverage in building their presence on the platform. The platform is owned by Meta/Facebook, and so the two share audiences, which can easily be linked together.

The company has been trying to spin-off into a long-form video platform akin to YouTube. This effort, first called IGTV and later Instagram TV, has been floundering for some time. The explosion of Tik Toc has pushed Instagram to redirect their video focus onto short form content. Known as "reels", they function in much the same manner as TicTok. Time will tell how that does for them.

Pinterest

Pinterest is particularly valuable for businesses because it is a place where visitors go to discover ideas and content. It is primarily image-based and was built as a sort of digital bulletin board. Users share images based on themes or topics. One of the biggest draws of Pinterest is how it caters to inspiration and brainstorming. For example, Pinterest is among the first places I to go to find ideas for landscape gardening. Searching for either of these terms returns a huge assortment of landscape and garden ideas. From there, the site displays a virtually endless scroll of relevant images. Despite being designed around browsing, Pinterest users come to the site to browse inspiration for specific interests. This makes it a prime social platform for brand-building, especially if you sell manufactured goods or services.

Show up where your customers are and not where you wish them to be.

Chapter 16: Managing Your Social Media Presence

Many businesses underestimate the effort it takes to maintain their social media and fail to allocate resources properly. Social audiences expect frequent content updates and will not be receptive to businesses perceived to have "abandoned" their accounts. Social platforms are always rolling out new ways to post content and connect with users. Competition between these companies is fierce – as is the competition between the businesses that use them for building their brands. Social media users are easily bored and distracted, so maintaining their attention is an unending war of attrition.

All businesses have limited resources, and only the largest can afford to maintain active presences on every social media platform they wish. Even so, few businesses are a fit for every platform due to their differences in audiences and contexts. Some business leaders let their egos drive them to adopt every new platform that comes along. Don't waste resources on social media that isn't a good fit for your company – invest in where your audiences are.

Expect to commit significant time to social media management. Even a modest social presence entails a part-time workload just to update and monitor posts. Content creation, especially for the more multimedia-heavy platforms, can become a full-time job. Some businesses opt to outsource their social media. There is a thriving social media management industry that caters to companies of all sizes. If you choose to go this route, understand that you will still need an in-house person to be a principal point-of-contact. Social media is far too critical to let an external firm have carte blanche over it. Ideally, if you can afford it, I recommend using in-house talent for this. External firms can be great but will not care as much about your reputation as you or your (well-treated) employees do. If you opt to manage your social media in-house, it pays to have backup content at the ready. This comprises pre-produced social content that you can pull from and post at any time. This inoculates you against any periods where your social media manager is unavailable – you will still have something to use to maintain a regular posting schedule.

Monitor, Listen, and Respond

Social media is not a set-it-and-forget-it affair – it exists for people to continuously share and communicate. All conversations on your social media posts are opportunities for you to connect with your audiences. These are opportunities to learn about them and their attitudes toward your brand. They are sharing their experiences with you, your products, and how they perceive them. This type of feedback is of immense importance to business intelligence and development.

In many cases, social audiences will be sharing positive things about you. Such praise is worth lauding and amplifying. Gratitude goes a long way in raising and celebrating this good will. In most cases, a simple "thank you" is enough. Particularly positive comments deserve a special response. In these cases, be sure to personalize the response and demonstrate that you read what they said and took it to heart. Positive social comments are valuable because they are trusted by other users. Amplifying these posts is well worth the effort. However, responses must be timely – social media is very "current", and it looks weird to respond to comments that are older than a day or two.

Inevitably, you are going to encounter less-than-positive comments and even outright negative sentiments. A little negativity can go a long way to eroding your reputation, and so every instance needs attention. Timeliness is especially important in responding to negative comments – you must display that you care about what is said and that you are accessible and reliable when things go bad.

There is a great deal of overlap with social media and customer service. In fact, it can be regarded as an intersection of public relations (PR) and customer service. Nobody likes bad or unresponsive customer service - when people see you ignoring negative comments it tells them that your customer service is bad. Refer to the section "Finessing Negative Content" from Chapter 14 on how to respond to negative online sentiments.

An additional consideration with negative social comments is how public you want the conversation to be after you have responded. Large or more complex problems are best handled off of social media, and so you should get them to continue the matter via email, chat, or phone. In cases where you have resolved a negative complaint, gently ask that they acknowledge your assistance - DO NOT beg or try to coax it from them. If you cannot effectuate this, at least leave a comment declaring that you have heard them and will try to take corrective action. Remember, you need to communicate that you are actively listening and responding.

Flaunt Your Authority

Nobody wants to do business with someone who doesn't know what they are doing. Social media is where you demonstrate your expertise and authority to the world. This is all about setting a narrative where you are an expert in your industry and associated subject matter. The best way to demonstrate expertise is to be helpful. Bragging will get you nowhere and will do more to harm than good to your reputation. Nobody likes braggarts.

Helpful expertise on social media comes down to two things: providing useful content and answering questions. Useful content is ostensibly practical and serves to solve problems. Useful content includes how-to guides, infographics, industry reports, and case studies. Explanatory content is also great for flaunting your expertise. Articles providing layperson explanations of complex concepts in your industry are particularly invaluable. Be sure to include ample callbacks to who you are and where else you can be found on the internet. As always, this content should link directly to your owned content pages – particularly on your website.

Answering questions on social media is another effective means of establishing subject expertise and authority. This requires you monitor social media for users posting questions or their problems related to your industry. Engaging in these conversations can be great for your reputation, but only if you present well. You must know what you are talking about and answer the questions with substance and clarity. As a business on social media, people know you are ultimately trying to promote yourself and will so scrutinize what you have to say. The challenge is on you to overcome such cynicism by providing useful expertise. Be sure not to come off as a bullshitter as people can smell that a mile away on social media. Be as genuine as possible.

Network With Others

Businesses can benefit from networking on social media. The first reason is optics: you need to demonstrate to the social audience that you are there to network like anyone else. This is especially true for small brands, which can appear genuine in a way that large companies simply cannot. Second, networking activities gets you more exposure and makes your business more compelling to follow. Networking bolsters the "human" element in your presentation and helps facilitate connections with potential customers. Users are much more likely to follow businesses on social media that provide more than glorified advertising. Finally, social networking creates opportunities to connect with influencers, authorities, and even your competitors. Good business sense demonstrates the value of fostering good will between competitors and similar brands. You never know what such relationships can bring to your business, and social networking is not unlike an online business networking party. Partnerships can emerge out of online networking just as they can from an in-person event.

Social networking activities entail sharing and engaging. It is highly unlikely you create all the content needed to cover every nuance of your industry. To fill these gaps, consider sharing content from other brands. After all, you would not be opposed to having other brands share your content in turn. Additionally, engaging in conversations topical to your industry help bolster your reach. Take care when entering conversations started by competitors – some can get understandably apprehensive at first. Gauge engagement wisely.

Foster Calls-to-Action

Once you have a strong social media presence, you can start using it to encourage customer actions. This is the part of your social media development that comprise your sales funnels. As part of these funnels, you utilize social media to put offers and enticements to get your audience to click-through and convert.

Social media is important because your network will likely have both potential and existing customers. Existing customers are especially valuable since they have already proven to be receptive to your brand. This creates opportunities to garner repeat business through cross-selling, replenishment selling, or upselling.

If you have your sales funnels fully synergized, your product offers will be appearing across your entire online presence. However, social networks are much more personal, and so bring you much "closer" to the customer. Consider using special promotions for your social networks. Gestures like this help strengthen the bond between social followers and your brand.

Just as social media is not owned media, neither are your followers there fully yours. The social platforms can remove you or your followers at any time - just as they could delete your posts and other content. To this end, you should be working hard to encourage your social followers to engage with your email newsletters. Given that social followers have already shown interest in your brand, they are likely to be interested in your newsletters. Since you own and control your email marketing lists, it is critical to have as much of your social audience as possible on it. Your social profiles should have permanent links to your email signup pages. In addition, you can create special posts and offers on your social media that encourage and reward signups.

The Importance of Consistency

When you have chosen your social media platforms, be prepared to commit to them. Having outdated, neglected, or abandoned social media is worse than having none at all. It communicates disinterest in customer outreach, poor business management, and make some people wonder if you went out of business. Only take on as many social media outlets as you can reasonably maintain with regular updates. Additionally, as the public can directly communicate and interact with you on social media, you will need to provide timely responses. This is why even small companies often have a dedicated social media manager on staff. As perhaps the most public-facing facet of your business, your social media presence must always look its best.

As with every other aspect of your online presence, your social media must be consistent with your branding and design. Your design elements such as logos and color schemes must match the rest of your online appearance. Remember that your website should set the tone for how all your branding appears online - see Chapter 2. Furthermore, do not neglect the importance of consistent *tone* in your social media presence. If your brand and company identity is laid back and fun, it needs to be represented in your social media.

A useful practice in maintain brand consistency is to maintain a branding style guide. This is your **brand bible** and describes every aspect of your design, graphics, typography, presentation, communication tone. Reference back to this document every time you are creating media posts or business profiles on your social media pages.

Tread Carefully and Plan Every Message

On the internet, it takes very little to ruin a business, and nothing can do more damage than a mistake on social media. In 2012, after the gun massacre in Aurora Colorado, the hashtag #Aurora was trending on Twitter. A small online clothing retailer posted a tweet saying: *"#Aurora is trending, clearly about our*

Kim K inspired #Aurora dress ;)" Obviously, this created a firestorm of backlash toward the company. The company did what many marketers do: they saw a trending hashtag on social media and used it to show up on user feeds. Being based in the UK, this company did not immediately know why #Aurora was trending, nor did they check to see why before posting. The tweet was taken down after an hour, but the damage had been done. Even apologies were too little, too late and their business will forever be associated with the tweet incident in search engines. The company has since renamed and rebranded.

The preceding story is a cautionary tale about the power of social media. As much as you might want to present an image of being cool and spontaneous, every single bit of media posted on social networks must be carefully planned. Social media moves so quickly that even bad posts that get taken down quickly can still do irreparable damage to your image. Internet culture is also notoriously sensitive and cynical. Nuance and subtlety are so difficult to express online that they can be regarded as nonexistent. Social media is essential to running an online business, but the risks are so great that it helps to be a bit paranoid.

A canny social media strategy must have protocols in place for every post you make. It should be consistent with your branding and tone. Above all, every post or reply should have multiple people reviewing it to ensure it is "safe" to go up.

Messaging must be clear and easy to understand with no room for it being misconstrued. It also helps to get a feel for the days' current trends and news cycle before anything is posted. Always be cautious and assume nothing.

Synergize Content with Social Media

Recall from Chapter 6 that your buyer journeys can take your audience across multiple marketing funnels. To maximize the chances for conversions, you must ensure the pathways your audiences take are unbroken. For most businesses, social media is the largest public-facing component of their operation. This necessitates you synergize your content with your social channels.

Never forget that the content you post to social media is not owned media – the social platform has ultimate power over it. They determine the rules for what you put there as well as who can see it and when. If you make social your primary outlet for your content, you run the risk of losing it. Your long-form content should always primarily exist on your website and other owned media locations like blogs.

Synergize your long-form media releases by posting links and snippets on social media. Every new blog post should be mirrored on your social channels. Offer snippets or summaries of the content with links to your pages. The ultimate goal with all your content is to get audiences to connect with *you*. Just as your paid advertising leads visitors to your website, so should your social media posts.

The reverse is also true for visitors to your owned website content. Every blog post, product listing, and content page should have easy ways for visitors to share them to social media. Most website platforms offer such features built in. In addition, every social media page platform you are on should be clearly and prominently linked on your website. Best practices place these links clearly at the beginning and end of your page content, or on the header of every page.

Curate everything you are about to say or post online. The internet never forgets.

Chapter 17: Paid Social Media

Social media companies make money by selling attention. They maximize their revenue by keeping users as engaged as possible on their websites and apps. This attention is the product they sell to advertisers and governments alike. More engagement equals more inventory for them sell.

The attention sold by social media is so valuable to marketers because of how effectively it can be targeted. Social platforms have incredibly detailed data on their users including demographics, interests, life circumstances, and personal connections. One of the perpetual challenges for marketers is getting their messaging in front of the right audiences. Because social platforms have such specific information on their users, it makes it easy to target distinct audiences with advertising. Social media effectively meets one of the big challenges in marketing: reaching audiences who are most likely to convert into customers.

Just as search is divided by organic vs. paid results, so too is social media. You can grow your social audience organically by posting quality content and active user engagement. You can also get social media exposure rapidly if you are willing to pay for it – just like paid search. As with search engines, you should be utilizing both approaches as part of a comprehensive social media strategy.

Paid social marketing does not principally sell followers or likes. They typically are built around promoting and pushing your content in front of targeted audiences. Social media platforms are dependent on users' perceptions of the communities they foster. If follower and like counts are shilled, then it diminishes the authenticity of the community. You might have encountered companies that purport to sell you social followers and likes. These are scams and run against the TOS of every social platform. Social companies constantly monitor for fakery, and if you get caught using one of these services, you can end up banned from the network. Bad news.

Social Media Ads vs Search Ads

A principal difference between search and social ads involves user agendas. Social media users are there to consume content based on interests. They are squarely in "browse" mode rather than "search" mode. As with display ads, your ads are competing with the content on the page for audience attention. However, in most cases social ads are displayed in a native format – they appear as integrated elements on the page.

Another key difference between paid search vs paid social ads lie in targeting. Social platforms categorize users by interests and demographics. Again, this is much like how a standard display network operates. Where search ads are based around bids on search keywords, social ads are based around bidding on audience interests. Your audience research and personas should be the basis for the demographics and psychographics you target your social bids on. In addition, if you are already seeing success on social media, the profiles of your followers can be used to formulate targeted campaigns to reach similar audiences.

Landing pages differ with paid social media ads as well. Depending on the platform or placement type, your landing pages might be your business profile page or specific social posts. Other placements can link directly to landing pages on your website. Again, it depends on the type of placement and its respective goal. The goals of social media ads are largely the same as your other calls-to-action. However, you should also strive to grow your social media presence with ads targeted specifically to grow your social followers and engagement. Remember that social followers can be incredibly valuable and receptive. It pays to target campaigns focused specifically on promoting your best content in the hope it will connect with users and compel them to follow you.

Types of Social Media Ads

Social media trends change constantly, and the platforms are always rolling out new ways to connect with audiences. This happens on both the "organic" and paid aspects of these networks. You will notice that paid social media frequently develop new ways to place content. In most cases, these are simply variations of existing methods. Regardless, boredom is the enemy of user engagement, so social networks deploy new ways for users to interact with content and advertisements.

Social media owes much of its success to the popularity of mobile devices, and so they place heavy emphasis on their respective apps. For this reason, most paid social media must be native or optimized for mobile. In many cases, certain types of paid placements only appear on the mobile version of the site. Your website should be mobile-friendly regardless of your business strategy. However, it *must* be mobile friendly if you intend to leverage social media advertising.

Display Ads

Display ads are advertisements placed on various elements of the social media website. These ads can be of just about any type of media including images or video. Social media in general is very audiovisual in focus, so you should minimize usage of text-only placements in your ad lineup. Most ads on social media take the native approach in placement.

Promoted Posts

A promoted post is one where you pay to have one of your existing social posts "boosted" to appear at the top of user feeds. These can appear in the feeds of either your followers or as suggested posts for non-followers based on their interests. Promoted posts typically appear as native placements with an indicator that it is a paid post. This type of paid social media is ideal for building up your base of followers because it gets your actual social posts in front of a larger audience.

In-Line Offers

These behave like shopping ads as seen on search display networks. You submit product listings to be social platform to be placed in users' feeds based on interest. Clicking on these ads will direct users to your product webpage for ordering. Social media platforms are increasingly offering the ability for users to purchase items directly from within the site or app itself,

Meet the Social Platforms, Again

In chapter 15, we looked at many of the leading social media companies and their contrasting approaches to social networking. This time, we will look at how they approach paid placements. Although they cater to different audience tastes, the way they handle paid placements have many similarities. In addition, social networks categorize their audiences under similar paradigms. The primary difference you will face if utilizing multiple social platforms for paid placements is the content. Your ads and promoted content on these sites must match the cultural paradigm of the social network. In most cases, paid social media uses the bid-auction approach seen in most other online advertising.

Meta AKA Facebook

As the largest social network, Facebook has the broadest and most robust social ad platform, known as **Meta for Business**. It allows for targeting based on a large array of demographic factors including age, gender, social connections, marital status, spoken languages, and even location. Moreover, you can target based on interest categories both broad and specific. A particularly useful feature is the ability to target users who have similar psychographics as your existing followers – a great way to bolster your follower count. Facebook is also big with ad retargeting – the practice of repeating ads in front of users who have shown some interest in your brand, product, or industry. This is implemented via a tracking pixel deployed on your website. Facebook also boasts an assortment of ad types and formats. These include images, videos, product placements, promoted posts, carousels (rotating arrays of images) and more.

Twitter

Twitter is known particularly for its fast-moving nature. Its approach to advertising tailors to this by focusing on promoting content instead of ad placements. On Twitter, you can pay to promote a tweet to a broader audience. Known as **sponsored tweets**, these tweets are given prominent placement on user feeds. You can also pay to have your entire twitter account promoted as a suggested follow for users who may be interested in you. Finally, Twitter lets you promote a trend that appears in the same place where trending topics appear to users. This is particularly useful for brand events like product launches or announcements. Paid placements on Twitter can be targeted by keywords or by interests based on who users follow. These can include order conversions or increasing your Twitter follower count.

Reddit

The self-organized nature of Reddit makes it quite easy to target ads based on audience interests. Reddit ads can be placed within specific subreddits and so can reach specific audiences with ease. It offers both promoted posts and standard native display ads. Additionally, Reddit offers conventional banner-style ads.

TikTok

TikTok is video platform, and as with your standard content, you will need to produce videos yourself. Audiences are targeted via demographic and interest categories. The principal ad type on TikTok are in-feed ads where your video ad is interspersed within user feeds. You can also pay more to have these ads show at the very top of the feed when the app is opened. If you have a ton of money, you can have your ad take over the entire app for all users every time they open it. TikTok also lets you promote special hashtags centered on your brand that encourage users to create related videos.

Paid or otherwise, the challenge with TikTok lies with resonating with the audience. Many marketers struggle figuring out how to connect with Gen-Z culture. This is exacerbated by TikTok being a video platform. Videos must be simple, entertaining, and authentic. Your content must fit with current trends and feel like a natural part of the culture. TikTok is a case in which partnering with an established influencer or creator is a good idea.

YouTube

Paid advertising on YouTube is managed via Google Ads and is used to either promote your own YouTube content or to place commercials within other videos. Audiences use the platform for both searching and browsing. YouTube caters to both usage types with robust search and a powerful suggestion algorithm. Audience targeting can be implemented with both keywords and demographic information. Video ads involve more time and resources than regular display ads since you need to produce your own video content.

There are two varieties of paid YouTube placements. The fist are standard display ads. These text or image ads appear either as ads within the YouTube site or as overlay ads that appear on the lower portion of a video. The other type is in-stream video ads. Known as *bumpers*, in-stream video ads can appear before, during, or after the main video and can run up to 30 seconds. These can be set to be skippable after 5 seconds or as completely un-skippable, which force the user to watch the entirety of the video. Users understandably hate non-skippable ads and using them could paint your brand in a negative light, so don't use them. Effective in-stream ads should be skippable but designed to be compelling enough to capture audience attention in 5 seconds or less.

LinkedIn

The unique value with LinkedIn ads is its targeting. Because it is a professional network, you can target based on work industry, company, job title, location, business size, and more. The professional context of LinkedIn, along with this powerful targeting, make it an excellent B2B advertising venue.

LinkedIn advertising consists of a standard ad display network paradigm. Ads can be placed as native elements, image carousels, and even as promoted or sponsored content. They can be formatted as text, images, or video. LinkedIn has functionality where you can create auto-populating webforms as landing pages – highly useful for lead-generation campaigns. LinkedIn also offers sponsored messaging ads, which appear in the personal inboxes of users as direct messages. These messages are designed to open lines of dialogue between you and the target audience.

Snapchat

The advertising features on Snapchat are very robust. Targeting is done by demographics, interests, devices, and location. Like Facebook, it can automatically generate target audiences based on your existing audience. The principal ad format on Snapchat are full-screen videos or images that intersperse between regular content. The video versions of these ads can be made non-skippable for up to 6 seconds. Snapchat also offers product listing ads in carousel format called *collection ads*. Their biggest contribution to social media was popularizing social stories, and so their ad offerings also allow for story ads. These are collections of ads served in 3-5 second intervals like a normal story. If you are interested in some more high concept advertising, Snapchat allows for branded image filters and stickers for users to use in their own posts.

Instagram

Instagram has a broad advertising suite. It offers display ads, promoted posts, an integrated shopping platform, and an influencer marketplace. Audience targeting is very powerful thanks to its shared data with Facebook, which is its parent company (AKA Meta). Instagram uses the promoted post model for paid placements, which boosts your existing content to new audiences.

Instagram Shopping is an integrated platform that allows brands to sell products directly within Instagram. Getting setup on Instagram Shopping involves uploading your product catalog or connecting your e-commerce website to the platform. Instagram Shops are found on your business profile page as well as being discoverable on the shopping section of the platform. Advertising your specific products is done by creating posts for your product, tagging it as a shopping post, and promoting it as you would a standard Instagram post.

Pinterest

Pinterest advertising works on the promoted post model, which they refer to as *promoted pins*. You pay to have your regular Pinterest content, or "pins" boosted to appear in front of target audiences in their feeds. Targeting is based on interests, follows, and demographics. You can also have Pinterest auto-generate suggested targets based on your existing audience. As with other follower-based social platforms, you can focus on either driving website/sales/app traffic or increase your brand awareness and follower count. Promoted pins can be utilized with the array of pin types available on the platform including stories, videos, and image carousels. Pinterest also joins the trend of social platforms offering in-app sales via *buyable pins*. They are setup in much the same as Instagram Shopping by way of product uploads or e-commerce website integration.

Managing Social Ad Platforms

You should be using the paid features of every social media platform your business is active on. This is essential for maximizing your reach on these platforms. Most social media ads platforms are based upon boosting your native social content – the posts are the ads themselves. Your best social posts deserve to get as much exposure as possible, both to your existing followers and to new audiences.

Many businesses mistakenly believe that the same people who create social media content are the best ones to manage social media ads. The skill set for creating good social content is not the same as running social media ads. Researching and targeting audiences and managing ad bids are marketing and analysis skills. Making social content is a creative skill. Even if you or your personnel have both talent sets, they still require time and focus to do right. Optimally, you should split these responsibilities between at least two people if you want to ensure each gets the attention they need. Obviously, they should still be working closely together and communicating regularly.

Every social media platform offers robust analytics suites for both social and advertising performance. Just as with your paid and organic search, your content and campaigns must be designed around achieving specific goals. On social media, these goals are typically focused on directing sales and sales leads on your website or building your base of followers on the social platform. To track your website-based goals, you will need to connect your site to the social media platforms. This is usually done by a tracking pixel placed in the source code of your site. Increasingly, social platforms can connect to e-commerce platforms directly through the website backend.

The same rules of management and improvement apply to paid social media as it does to your search advertising as outlined in Chapter 10 and Chapter 11. Every campaign is designed to achieve specific objectives. Ads and promotions that do not perform well should get reworked or deleted outright. Apply the laws of natural selection to your social campaigns, ads, and promotions: the successful ones survive while the unsuccessful ones perish.

The Rising Tide of Data Privacy Concerns

Online privacy is becoming more of an issue every year, and scrutiny on social media will only increase in the eyes of both the public and governments. Social media is not going anywhere, but it is destined to see big changes down the road. Social and search platforms can both be directly integrated with most leading e-commerce platforms. These e-commerce platforms can further integrate with an assortment of CRM (customer relationship management) services such as Salesforce. This can create a vast and powerful confluence of personal data – even for relatively small businesses. It is highly advisable you stay abreast of developments in the data privacy space regarding your responsibility with your data and how you use it. This is especially true if you export any of this data from their respective platforms and do additional analysis on it. A wave of regulations is coming in the vein of GDPR that will place limits on how you can analyze or "process" this information. This is to say nothing of the ever-present danger that lies in company data breaches that happen every day. You are liable for the security of your information, or lack thereof. As lawyers say: "govern yourself accordingly".

"That depends...on how well your manners are, and how big your pocketbook is." – 'Dexter Jettster' – from Star Wars

---

PART VI: The Online Landscape

Chapter 18: Relationship Management

Acquiring new customers is seldom easy nor cheap. For any business to be sustainable, it must build and maintain long-term relationships with customers. The internet has been a boon for customer-business relationships. The convenience of the internet has brought buyers and sellers together more than any time in history. Furthermore, communications channels have never been more open, and the concept of waiting for stores to open or phones to be answered are relics of the past.

The rise of online commerce has not been without its drawbacks. The internet has brought so many competitors and customers into the fray that many voices can get lost in the noise. Even relatively small online businesses often struggle with high email/chat volumes. Businesses must also contend with customers who are more empowered now than ever thanks to the internet. While positive word-of-mouth can spread quickly online, so too can negativity. Unlike in the pre-web days, a single angry or vindictive customer can greatly harm a company– especially small ones. This can be especially frustrating because the internet seldom cares about what is true - particularly in matters of customer sentiment. For customers, the choice and convenience of internet shopping came at a price: privacy. More than ever, consumers are tracked online by websites, browsers, and their own devices. This data feeds huge AI systems that can surmise a huge amount of information about consumers private lives. We are now at a point where machine learning can make predictions on the future behavior of individuals with unsettling accuracy.

Transactional vs Relationship Marketing

There is a contrast between relationship and transaction-focused marketing. The principal difference lies with timescales. Quick entry, quick exit operations are focused on doing whatever they need to get sales quickly. The same is true for many businesses that offer one-off products or services. The emphasis of transactional marketing are product features and immediacy. Transactional business is based on little to no direct customer contact, especially after the sale.

Relationship marketing takes a long-term perspective. The post-sale benefits of the product are emphasized – especially in terms of quality and customer support. Businesses that sell high-cost or replenishable products are especially dependent on relationship marketing to thrive. Relationship marketing necessitates a higher degree of contact between business and customers before and after a sale.

The Importance of Relationships

Depending on the product you are selling, the marketing cost to acquire an average customer is likely very high compared to the net sale price. Under many business models, a single sale cannot always cover the cost of generating it. The only way to sustain such a business is to maximize the value of existing customers. This comes in the form of repeat business as well as their goodwill and positive influence on other potential customers. Customer goodwill is highly trusted online and can effectively help bring in additional customers. Customers acquired this way enter much "lower" on the sales funnel and thus cheaper to acquire. This in turn drives down the overall cost of obtaining customers. Reductively, this is all there is to relationship management: maximize the value of your customers and drive down the cost of attracting new ones.

Trust is the currency of all customer-business relationships. The higher the cost of your goods, the more trust a customer likely will to feel before making an expensive sale. The more valuable your customers are, the more trust you will need to cultivate in order to keep them. What is trust? For customers, it is the sense that the brand they are spending their money on will stand by their product and be receptive to their needs – especially if things go wrong with the product. In addition, customers want to feel appreciated for their business. Just as businesses forment trust to maximize the value of customers, customers wish to maximize the value they obtain from the goods they purchase. A product/service that has the full backing and support of the brand is more valuable to consumers than those who do not. They are often willing to pay more for a good if it is seen as having higher intrinsic value. This applies to more than just physical quality, but also the level of post-sales support the customer can expect.

Relationships are based primarily on emotions. It is a matter of how customers feel about brands that form the basis of trust and loyalty. Their relationship with your brand needs to feel like they are connecting with people rather than some faceless entity. This is a basic human tendency and is why even AI chatbots have human names. Its why Alexa has been so successful. The best business relationships are about *connecting* with customers in a way that resembles one-on-one human connections.

The emotional aspect of customer-business relationships is also why negative experiences can be so damaging. We all have basic expectations about how an online sales experience should be: Find product; put in cart; checkout; payment; confirmation page; email receipt; ship notification; delivery; enjoy the product. We tend not to think much about this process if it goes smoothly, and so the experience is emotionally neutral. However, if one or more of these steps goes poorly, it presents an unexpected inconvenience and creates attendant negative emotions. On the internet, customer displeasure can be immediately expressed via multiple channels. People seldom post to Facebook about how their online purchase was "normal". Problematic purchase experiences are another story and can spread through social conversations like wildfire.

Customer Relationship Concepts

Cultivating good customer relationships is a cornerstone of good business. As with every other large body of knowledge, the best way to begin understanding it is to familiarize yourself with the basic concepts and nomenclature. There is also an assortment of services available to help manage your customer relationships such as Salesforce, Microsoft Dynamics, and Adobe Marketing Cloud. As your business grows, you should consider investing in one of these services. To properly evaluate these options for the best fit for your operation, you must know the lingo. Below are some important concepts and terminology in maintaining customer relationships:

Customer Relationship Management (CRM)

CRM is the blanket term for the organization, management, and strategy utilized in fostering customer relationships. Specifically, it is focused on efforts to maximize sales from existing customers and keep them engaged with the brand for as long as possible.

Customer Acquisition Cost (CAC)

How much do you need to spend to get a new customer? This is a critical question to ask when planning your marketing strategies. At its most basic, it calculated by dividing your marketing costs by the number of new customers over a set time. For example: If you spend $1000 for marketing in one month and got 100 new customers, your CAC is $10. This metric is useful only if you fully understand its nuance. First, you must ensure that the assessment of your marketing costs is accurate. It goes beyond your ad spend, and includes your technical, labor, and production costs. Ads, copy, images, and video content take resources to create. Similarly, the time spent designing and setting up your marketing campaigns need to be considered. Another thing to think about is the right timeframe to make this calculation. Short-term CACs are unreliable as it takes time to build sufficient marketing exposure to build enough data to properly quantify. You also need to be aware of the time between a customer first interacts with your marketing and when they convert. This is known as customer **latency**.

Customer Lifetime Value (CLV)

Customer Lifetime Value is the metric that describes how much your customers spend with your company over the course of their active lifetime. In this case, **customer lifetime** means the period between their first and last spend with your company. The simplest version of this metric is calculated by taking the average annual revenue per customer multiplied by the average customer lifespan. For Example: If your average customers spend about $500 per year and your average customer lifespan is 3 years, then your CLV is $1500. You can go further with this and subtract your average CAC cost – preferably as it was at the time the customer was first acquired. Deeper dives into this metric can also subtract overhead costs associated with maintaining contact with the customer. Strategically, CLVs dictate how much you can afford to invest in a single customer – from acquisition to maintenance and service.

As with all such metrics, you need to understand the subtleties behind it. For one thing, determining what constitutes a "dead" customer is not always clear. Unless you have clinching proof that they are not coming back, it is not uncommon for customers to take "breaks" from purchasing only to come back years later. Depending on your product or service, there might be different expectations for how frequent conversions would be:

customers can be expected to reorder coffee pods on a monthly basis, but certainly not car tires.

CLVs can also be broken out into segments among your customer base. This can be done in any number of ways depending on the specificity of your customer data. You may find that certain customer demographics have higher CLVs than others. This is important information to know and should be a big part in how you refine your customer persona models.

Churn Rate

Your churn rate is useful in measuring the efficacy of your brand in keeping customers happy and engaged – higher churn rates are bad news. This metric measures the percentage of customers who end their business relationship with a company. The calculation is made by dividing the number of customers who left a company during a time divided by the total number of customers at the beginning. For Example: If you started last year with 1000 customers and 100 ended their relationship with you during that time, your churn rate was 10%. Churn rates are notoriously tricky to calculate. As with CLV, determining what constitutes a "dead" customer is not always easy. This is easier to know if your product is sold under a subscription or contract basis. Single order products can be more of a challenge.

Regaining lost customers can be difficult - depending on why they left. Some customers simply go dormant and can be brought back for less than your average CAC. Those who left because of a negative experience are much more challenging to bring back. For these customers, your task is to understand what went wrong and ensure it does not happen to current and future customers.

To contend with a high churn rate, you must understand the reasons. This starts by asking questions. Utilize customer surveys and questionnaires on a regular basis. Monitor social media for unhappy customers. Ensure your website has clear places to leave feedback on every page. You can also contact lapsed customers directly to ask what went wrong. Take care to not be too intrusive - making them even more upset will only make things worse.

Relationships Start with Business Practices

Businesses that thrive long-term do so in part because they cultivate good relationships with their customers. These connections are understood to be essential to the success and survival of the business and are not treated as afterthoughts. The more a business nurtures its customer relationships, the more resilient and stable it generally is. It costs far less to market and sell to existing customers than it does to find new ones. Better relationships with customers not only keep them around, but it raises their overall value to the business.

Customer relationships must be at the center of your business culture. Your company must operate as a customer-oriented operation, focusing on their two principal needs: product quality and customer support. Great customer support is synonymous with trust – you stand by your product and are committed to ensuring expectations are met.

Customer support is often regarded as beginning only after a sale has been made. Not true. Customer support is part of the complete customer experience. For online businesses, this encompasses the entirety of a visitors' experience with your website. Ease of use, navigability, security, and clarity are important features of a great site – all acting in symphony to ensure the visitor has the easiest time possible finding what they are looking for. A customer-focused website must have clear pathways for visitors to find help if they run into any trouble or confusion.

A customer-oriented business builds trust in their brand by offering full product support. New customers take a risk whenever they do business with a new company. Assurances that any problems with their purchase will be promptly addressed will go a long way toward alleviating hesitation. Delivering on customer service issues bolsters your reputation and trustworthiness, resulting in more new customers willing to take a chance with you.

Relationships are Built Through Communication

Cultivating customer relationships is done through active communication. This happens on multiple levels. First, you need to be listening on every channel where customers (and non-customers) are talking about you. Monitor social comments, forum posts, online reviews, and anywhere else these conversations happen. Take to heart everything that is said and respond when and where appropriate.

Good customer service requires open and accessible lines of communication – it must be as easy as possible for a customer to reach you. Few things turn off customers more than being unable to reach someone for assistance. Your lines of communication must be multi-faceted, as people have different communication needs and preferences. Your website should have clear, unambiguous links on every page that lead to your support pages. In addition, your product, checkout, and account pages should have prominent links and messaging about where to go for help. Customers who find themselves stuck at checkout are likely to leave and never come back. Minimize this by making sure they can get in touch with you immediately!

With the internet, there are many communication channels by which customers can businesses. If you have the resources, try to utilize as many types as you can. You want to ensure you are accommodating as many communication preferences as possible. Most importantly, every one of these channels must be regularly monitored. Every message must be responded to – no matter what. Having unanswered or unacknowledged messages is worse than having no communication channels at all.

Email

Email is the ubiquitous standard for communicating with a business. Everywhere you are present online should have your email address clearly displayed. Every alternative form of communication you utilize should also provide your email contact as a backup.

Every email sent to your business must be answered promptly. Most internet users are accustomed to maximum response times of 24 hours or next business day. Ideally, you should aim to provide email responses within hours if you have the bandwidth. In any case, it is wise to setup your email client to auto-respond to messages confirming receipt of emails – it provides assurance to the sender that it did not go down a digital black hole.

If you face a large volume of messages, you can pre-sort your messages. This can be done in two ways. The first is using email subject lines, which can be sorted and filtered by most email clients. You can configure the links to your email to pre-fill the subject link in the HTML code. This way, you can have separate email links for different types of reasons a customer might need to contact you: "order problem", "product query", "sample request", etc. The other pre-sorting method is to have separate email addresses for your different types of queries: ordersupport@[yoursite],   productquery@[yoursite], samples@[yoursite].

The above methods of pre-sorting your contact email makes it easier for you to prioritize responses. In any case, when facing a volume of emails, prioritizing them is the most effective approach. Existing customers must be taken care of first. The next biggest priority are customers experiencing technical or logistical issues on your site. The specifics of your business and customer base will dictate the rest of your priority hierarchy. The least urgent of these are typically positive comments and compliments. Though they are not pressing matters like the rest, be sure to acknowledge and thank every single one. These customers are often happy to have their compliments reused for promotional purposes (without their identity divulged, obviously), and so you should always ask permission. Don't forget to ask them to leave positive reviews.

Online Contact Forms

Online forms are ways for customers to send you an email without having to go through their email client. In most cases, conversations started on embedded forms continue as standard email threads. Aside from user convenience, forms allow for them to provide more specific information. Forms are robust and can include input fields including subject, order info, name, email, dates, etc. Many website platforms allow for contact forms to autofill information from users who are logged in to the site.

Online forms are a favorite tool for businesses to generate sales leads on websites. They are easy to setup on as most website platforms have these built in. There are also many free tools to build your own, such as Google Forms. Bear in mind that if you utilize forms that collect submitted information in a database, you should make sure your website privacy and terms of use have language to reflect this method of data collection.

On-Site Chat

Customers love immediacy, especially when they have questions of problems. On-site chat clients cater directly to this. This type of chat client exists as an overlay on your website where customers can text directly with someone at your company. There are many chat services available and are relatively easy to deploy on most websites. On your end, you will be able to see where on your site the customer is– making it easy to render quick assistance if they are having technical issues.

The drawback to chat is a direct consequence of its benefit – you must ensure your chats are constantly manned and able to respond immediately. It is why many sites have open hours for their chat. You probably have encountered websites that have chat clients that never seem to be open. Smaller companies tend not to have the time and personnel to properly dedicate to chat. In most cases, the employees who are handling site chat are also the ones answering phones and emails.

Chatbots

When you do not have the human capacity, why not let a robot do it? This is the idea behind chatbots. On the customer side, chatbots function just like regular chat. They can click on any page on your site and open a chat dialogue. The difference, of course, is that they are conversing with artificial intelligence.

Chatbot AI is not truly intelligent, and functions more as a text parser than anything else. In this context, parsing is where the AI picks apart the user messages to determine what they are saying. Chatbots are built upon logic trees. You seed your chatbot with the types of questions you expect to get from users, and then set the various yes/no conditions that lead to the most appropriate answer. These are essentially the same question/answer protocols most human customer service representatives use – if you have such protocols, you already have a framework for seeding a chatbot.

Chatbots are effective when used within the scope of their abilities. Think of them as interactive FAQ pages and nothing more. Chats should be able to direct users to answers to standard support questions quickly. Everything else should be promptly directed to other communications channels manned by real people. The more a customer is trapped in a looping conversation with a bot, the more frustrated they will become.

Social Messaging

Part of good customer communication is being on channels they are comfortable with. To accommodate this, many businesses use the chat features on social media as their principal contact channels. The most popular are Facebook Messenger, Snapchat, and WhatsApp. Social messaging apps are an increasingly common way for people to communicate – they are available for free, integrate with their social networks, and are easy to use.

As social messaging services grow in ubiquity, so do audience expectations. If you are on a social media platform, users will increasingly expect for you to also be using its associated chat features. Ensure that social chat is part of your overall social media monitoring and listening plan. Even if you do not plan on making a social messenger your primary communication channel, you cannot risk having any messages go unanswered.

Phones

Though younger audiences are more comfortable with online communication channels, telephones are still the preferred method of communication for many people. In addition, a phone number helps add to the perception of legitimacy to an online business. Regardless, the rise of alternative communication channels continues to shift phones from being a business requirement to more of a perk. If you decide to field a phone number, it must be monitored and answered. If someone calls your business, they are expecting to talk to a *person*, not a recording.

Maintaining Engagement

Just like any long-term commitment, your relationship with your customers is an ongoing process. It unfolds across numerous channels and venues. Your customers can exist on various parts of their buyer journeys within multiple marketing funnels. Therefore, your outreach to must be holistic and span everywhere your online operation touches.

Accessibility

At every part of your online presence, you must be accessible to your customers. These are where you establish touchpoints with your audience, as covered in Chapter 6. All roads must lead to open communication channels. This includes every page, social post, blog entry, email, and advertisement you put out. At no point should a user feel they do not have a way to get in touch with you. Every touchpoint a customer has with your brand must include a way to reach you.

Personalization

Customers respond positively to personalization. They want to be treated like individuals and not some arbitrary number. Any direct interaction with customers must be done in a manner where they are treated like they are valued and understood. Terse, rude, or even ambivalent tone in interactions go against this. When you send out emails, they should be addressed to the recipient directly. Nearly every email newsletter provider has this functionality built-in, as do CRM systems. Your manual responses should strive to use real names in a conversational tone.

By now, you should understand that digital advertising can be narrowly targeted to specific audience profiles. Every campaign you create should have its ad content catered to the unique aspects of your target audience. As you will have crafted this targeting based on your personas, so too will your ads. Design your ads as if it was made just for your target personas.

Email Newsletters

Email marketing is one of the oldest types of online relationship marketing. The beauty of email newsletters is that they are opt-in media: the recipient has given clear interest and permission to receive marketing materials. Additionally, tracking metrics is easy to do with email newsletters. Messages can be tracked for opens, clicks, and conversions. Email lists are very easy to target to specific customers and demographic/interest groups for personalized campaigns. Nearly all internet users are familiar with the practice of email newsletters and are relatively comfortable with engaging with them. The email newsletter industry is one of the oldest on the internet, and so the top service providers have made it very easy to use. Of these, Mailchimp is the one I recommend the most.

Rewarding Loyalty

If you can calculate your customer lifetime vales (CLV), then you know who your most loyal customers are. These are the ones who order the most frequently and most reliably. They are the most valuable customers you have and should be celebrated and rewarded. This can be done with periodic discounts and gifts. Furthermore, these cream-of-the-crop customers should be periodically contacted directly to express your gratitude and to ensure they are still happy with your brand. Just as your unhappy customers can teach you what you are doing wrong, your satisfied customers can tell you what you are doing right – in fact, many can quite be quite eager to offer their advice.

Loyalty programs are easier than ever to deploy online. Many e-commerce platforms have built-in loyalty functionality. You can also employ one of the many third-party loyalty services that can integrate with your website. There are several different approaches to loyalty programs. These can include rewards points, customer spending tiers (spend more, get better perks), and paid loyalty programs (modeled after Amazons' Prime). The best fit for your company comes down to the preferences of your customers and the nature of your products.

One of the trendy types of customer loyalty management is known as **gamification**. This is the application of videogame mechanics into non-gaming contexts. For online businesses, these mechanics principally revolve around progression tracking. Examples of this include customer levels, badges, and missions. Progression is tracked via points that are earned as customers perform various actions such as placing orders, sharing brand content, referring others, leaving reviews, and more. As customers earn points, they progress through the game ranks. Points can be redeemed for discounts, free gifts, and more. Gamification provides visual representation of progress customers are making toward these rewards – playing to the emotional lure of making strides toward a goal. Gamification is not for everybody but is uniquely appealing to younger customer bases who have familiarity and comfort with videogame dynamics.

Leveraging Automation

The reach of the internet enables businesses to reach more audiences than ever before. This is great for business opportunities, but also can create a huge volume of messages, user accounts, and leads. Such volumes can prove to be insurmountable without employing automated processes. At every level of an online operation, there are features and services that can streamline your processes. Most email clients have automatic forwarders and sorting based on message criteria. Website platforms can connect to analytics, social media, CRM systems, and other Enterprise software.

There is an entire class of online services that exist automate digital processes. These services include the likes of IFTTT, Zapier, and Automate.io. They can connect to a huge array of software, online platforms, websites, and more to automate huge assortment of tasks. These automations are easy to configure and are based on simple program logic. Furthermore, they can help bridge together assorted platforms and services that might not have built-in connections to each other.

Customer Extension

As you are in business to make money, there are two things you want your existing customers to do: Spend more money and encourage others to do the same. Getting good word-of-mouth from existing customers is a matter of keeping them happy through quality and service. It can also be effectuated through referral incentives and rewards.

Existing customers are already actively purchasing with you, but you need not leave it at that – there are things you can do to boost and maximize this activity. This is known as **Customer Extension** and is the practice of expanding the buying behavior of your existing customers. This can be done in several ways.

Cross-selling is a tried-and-true technique where you promote products that are similar or complimentary to those your customer already buys. Cross selling opportunities can be deployed at the points-of-purchase on your website, either as suggested items while users browse or during checkout. You can also target your email marketing campaigns to customers based on complimentary products to their recent purchases.

Similarly, if your products are in a tiered pricing structure, you can engage in **Upselling**. Upselling encourages customers to upgrade to more expensive products as an alternative. It is important for these upgrades to be of clearly higher value. Incentives such as discounts go a long way here, as the customer had already decided on the lower-cost product for a reason. Your messaging must emphasize the extra value of the product and the "use it or lose it" immediacy of the discount offered.

"Rest assured I was on the internet within minutes registering my disgust throughout the world" – 'Comic Book Guy', from the Simpsons

---

Chapter 19: Putting Everything Together

The internet and associated technology like smartphones fundamentally transformed commerce and marketing. In a few short years, the immediacy of interactions between customer and business went from slow to instantaneous. The sheer number of available customers and competitors increased exponentially. For marketers, the most challenging change had to do with complexity. In the old days, there were a limited number of advertising and communication channels to contend with. Suddenly, networks upon networks of online audiences sprung up. Different types of adverting and social communication venues seemingly emerged every few months.

As the internet matured, an immense number of websites, forums, and communities emerged to cater to countless different audiences. What had once been a set of broad channels had splintered into countless smaller ones. Within these venues are multiple types of media ranging from text to images to videos. These various permutations of media are all used in different ways and contexts. Thus, internet media is complex, diverse, and fragmented. The same can be said about how users approach the internet – the average internet user can be part of any number of different online audiences.

Integrating Online

Before continuing, let's review some important concepts and terminology. First is the **persona**, a hypothetical person who represents a key segment of your target audience. Next is the **customer journey**, which is the roadmap a user (or persona) takes from the first time they are aware of your brand until they either convert to a customer or forget you forever. A **funnel** describes specific steps of progression a customer takes toward converting. Finally, a **channel** is a specific marketplace in which your products are promoted or sold.

More than ever, the internet has made business and brand marketing a holistic affair. A potential customer can encounter dozens of different forms of media every day. Additionally, a person might be part of multiple online audiences - depending on how much of their life is online. We all have aspects of our lives that express different parts of the same person: personal, professional, sexual, hobbyist, activist, etc. Each of these aspects can be catered to through the internet and the communities it fosters.

Though each online customer journey, a person might enter and exit multiple sales funnels. This happens as their internet browsing journeys pass through the communities, sites, and media they consume. The more integrated a persons' life is with the internet, the more funnels they pass through on their journeys. The younger your target audience is, the more likely they are to shift through different funnels. This fragmentation of the typical internet experience means a potential customer could fall off their customer journey into a dead end.

An effective online marketing strategy must ensure that fragmentation does not interrupt buyer journeys. This is achieved by employing two tactics. The first is to ensure your brand is present everywhere your target audiences go online. Knowing where to be is the result of good research on your target customers and personas. The other tactic is to accommodate and facilitate customers jumping between funnels. This is achieved by synergizing every aspect of your online operation through consistent branding and cross-linking. For instance, someone who finds your brand on social media and later a blog post should immediately recognize them as being of the same brand.

Going Offline

Depending on the specifics of your brand and customers, offline can still be a significant component of your marketing strategy. Businesses that have local reach, physical stores, or older customer bases are particularly good fits for offline marketing.

Offline promotion is understandably referred to as "traditional" media. It includes newspapers, print magazines, catalogues, flyers, radio, television, and billboards. Offline media can be great for building brand awareness with the right audiences – for many older consumers (who hold more wealth than younger people), offline is seen as a mark of legitimacy over online-only entities.

There are several drawbacks to offline media. It's expensive and comparatively worse at audience targeting than online media. Offline media is harder to personalize and can only offer as much information as the physical media allows. Offline advertising is notoriously difficult to track in terms of efficacy and ROI. As this book is focused on online marketing, the specifics on choosing and creating specific offline media is outside its scope. However, there are still digital considerations you need to make even when utilizing offline media.

The internet is the present and future of business and so your offline advertising must have hooks to your website. This ensures cross-funnel synergy in your marketing setup. It also can help address one of the big shortcomings of offline marketing: trackability.

The first thing to do with your offline media is to prominently feature your website URL. You should use a special web address just for your offline ads that lead to a special landing page for these audiences. This can be anything from a specific subpage or even a custom domain name. You can use your page analytics to attribute any traffic from these landing pages to their corresponding offline ads. Since these landing pages exist only to serve offline traffic sources, be sure to prevent search engines from indexing the pages. This can be achieved with "noindex" robots tags on each of these pages.

A handy tool for bridging offline to online media are **QR codes**. These are scannable images that smartphones can read that typically link to websites or apps. Utilize QR codes on your print media so people can access your landing pages directly from their phones. QR codes can be generated for free. There is also a paid variety of QR code called **dynamic QR**. These codes enable you to capture data about scans such as number, location, and device.

Another method of offline attribution is to offer specific coupon or discount codes in your ads. When customers use them, you can trace the sale and customer directly to the corresponding offline ad. Bear in mind that these discount codes must be identical due to the nature of print. This is rarely an issue so long as the code is compelling sales, but for tracking purposes, it is possible they could "leak" online if someone posts it. If this happens, much of the offline ad tracking you extrapolate becomes unreliable. It helps to monitor the internet for instances when these codes leak online so you know when such tracking is compromised.

Revisiting the Online Landscape

The landscape an online business operates in can be broken into five general areas: website, search, social media, external websites, and offline. Every single area requires extensive work and fine-tuning if your business is to realize its full potential. A complete online marketing strategy is not realized unless every one of these areas is addressed. Recall that customers move across these aspects of the internet all the time as they shift from one marketing funnel to another. Every area is thus connected and so your marketing must synergize them together.

These five areas of the online landscape can be categorized as one of four categories of media. These categories describe the nature and the level of control you have over them. They are derived from the **PESO model**: Paid, earned, shared, and owned. Paid media is anything you pay to have created and/or placed. Earned media is unpaid coverage you get from blogs, news, and word-of-mouth. Shared media is social media content that is shared among those communities. Owned media is any content that you control every part of – its creation, curation, and placement.

Your Website

Your website is the center of your online marketing world. It is likely the only place on the internet you fully control, including its data, content, and design. The website is where you set the basis for your brand identity from design all the way to tone. If you are an e-commerce operation, your site is also where your customer buying experience takes precedent – it must be functional and focused on accommodating their needs both during and after checkout.

Search Engines

Customers generally use the internet in one of two modes: search and browse. Search is where they are trying to find information to solve specific problems. Search engines are where you target audiences who are actively seeking the products and services that you provide. There are two sides to search: organic and paid. Organic searches show the most relevant results for what the user is looking for. Paid search is where you bid on keywords to come up for relevant searches. Both organic and paid search need to be utilized if you are to maximize traffic to your site.

Social Media

Social media is the dominant form of social communication and online community building. There are many varieties of social media that cater to different tastes. The currency of social networks is shares, likes, and follows. Nearly every social network has a company profile page that acts as the central hub for your presence on said network. Paid social media principally revolves around paying to have your social posts promoted to be in front of new audiences. Influencers are high-profile social media users with clout over large numbers of followers. They can promote your company for free if they like you (earned media) or for a fee (paid media).

External Websites

The rest of the internet can also be subcategorized based on the PESO model. External paid media sites include all ad spend outside of search engine and social media ad networks. These include affiliates, sponsorships, display networks, and non-social influencers. External earned media sites include news sites, blogs, journal articles, and online reviews. Outside of social networks, the most common shared media are found on blog comments, message boards, and assorted online communities. Finally, owned external sites are any websites you control that are separate from your main company website. This can include microsites and external company blogs.

Measuring Results

The online portion of all businesses exist to foster, support, and grow their operations. The internet is so dominant in commerce that few can survive or even exist without being online in some capacity. The extent to which a business should be online varies and is dependent on the company and its product. Whatever the case, businesses do not setup websites or social media for fun – they do so to make money

How do you know if your online strategy is worth it? How can you know if your online performance is optimal, or if it can do better? These are separate (but related) questions that address your overall business success. The answer ultimately comes down to the online return on investment, or **ROI**. Determining your online ROI is dependent on your goals. Typically, goals center on generating online sales or sales leads. Other goals can include fostering brand awareness, social follows, or other conversions like sign-ups or downloads. Measuring each requires you determine the value of each. Figuring some of these values is quite easy, as a conversion or sale are simple to track and quantify. Other metrics, like the value of an average sales lead or social follow require a bit more analysis.

Once you know the goal you are trying to measure, you must next figure out the cost of your online strategy. Website hosting costs, ad spend, and other paid promotions are easy to quantify. You must also factor in labor costs for programming, design, content creation, clerical work, social monitoring, and online customer service. You should be tracking these costs and metrics with as much specificity as possible – it lets you drill down deeper into your analysis to single out the ROI for specific parts of your operation. Knowing the ROI for your website, social media, ad spend, etc. are critical to determining where you need to improve or cut back on.

ROI is just the starting point in knowing how things are going with your online business. Even the smallest operation can access huge amounts of performance data. Between native analytics within website platforms, third-party trackers like Google Analytics, PPC analytics, social media analytics, offline enterprise software, and many more, you will have no shortage of data.

Key Performance Indicators (KPIs)

KPIs, or **Key Performance Indicators**, are the metrics you use to assess your performance in achieving your business goals. It is critical that your KPIs are specific and unambiguous. They must measure critical aspects of your business that determine its success and ability to sustain itself. KPIs must be quantifiable in that they can be specifically measured.

Additionally, KPIs must be actionable. To be an actionable metric, it must be something that you have influence over. For instance, you cannot control the weather (even if it affects your business), so it cannot be a KPI. For online businesses, KPIs commonly involve website metrics, sales, search rankings, and marketing performance.

Traffic Metrics

For many businesses, and certainly all in e-commerce, their website is the center of their online strategy. The most important measures of success have to do with traffic and conversions. These go hand-in-hand, and if things are optimized properly, more visitors should equal more conversions. Ideally, you are trying to direct quality visitors to your site and not just sheer quantities.

There are several ways to track web traffic. Most website platforms have built-in traffic analysis suites that can be quite effective. There is also Google Analytics, which is the most popular traffic tracking service. It is free and connects to nearly every major social and web platform out there. As Google is the largest search and PPC provider of all, the unity of this data makes it a must-have analytics solution.

Visitors

Visitors is the number of people who have come to your site over a period of time. The base metric counts anytime someone enters the site. Another metric called **unique visitors** counts the unique users who came to your site. They tell slightly different stories. A high proportion of visitors to unique visitors suggests a high amount of repeat visits to your site – a metric known as **returning visitors**. Conversely, a higher ratio of unique visitors suggests fewer users are returning to your site.

Pages per visit

This metric measures how extensively a visitor looks at your site. Higher pages per visit can suggest many things. On one hand, it may indicate visitors find your content compelling enough to look around. It can also mean that they are trying to find content and are not having an easy time of it. Google Analytics also provides tracking of visitors through your site, so you can see which pages they visit and in which sequence.

Exit Pages

Exit pages are the final page a visitor views before clicking away from your website. Nobody stays forever on a website, but if you have certain pages that are disproportionately driving traffic away at a higher proportion, it may be problematic.

Bounce Rate

Bounce rates describe the percentage of visitors who view a single page on your website and leave immediately. A high bounce rate is bad news – it is a sign that you are bringing in uninterested visitors to your site or that your content is of poor quality.

Session Length

Session length measures the time visitors stay on your website across all pages they visit. Compelling websites tend to keep peoples' attention longer.

Traffic Source

Traffic source data is an immensely useful. It indicates where your visitors are coming from when they enter your site. You can have many different sources that get listed in your analytics. However, your largest and most important referring sites should be clear. This is the principal data that helps you determine which sources produce the most interested in visits to your site. In addition, you can see how much of your traffic is **direct traffic**, which are incoming visitors who input your URL directly and do not come from a referrer. Direct traffic indicates visits who are neither search nor referrals.

Conversions

Conversion metrics describe customer actions. They are most used to measure sales but can be applied to any desired call-to-action from the customer. These can be newsletter sign-ups, sales leads, downloads, and more. Each call-to-action can be configured as a goal in Google Analytics. This lets you track separate conversion rates for each of your goals.

Tracking conversion rates are immensely important for paid and social marketing. They indicate how successful your website is at getting visitors who clicked on your ads or social posts to convert. These metrics were discussed in detail back in Chapter 10.

Audiences

Google Analytics enables you to track specific types of audiences based on attributes you define. This is useful for measuring the efficacy of your efforts to attract and convert specific types of visitors. Audiences can be grouped by demographics and interests. From there, you can run traffic analysis based on these segmented groups. This is especially useful in testing your online personas and how receptive they are to your content and marketing efforts.

Beyond Metrics

Monitoring business metrics is an important practice in determining what is going right and wrong with your business. Many businesses make the mistake of being overly reactive to their metrics - making rapid changes in response to sudden changes. Conversely, some ignore analytics and become comfortable with their business status quo – unaware that they are in the midst of an impending, yet avoidable, downturn. The nuance in utilizing business intelligence is developing the knack for recognizing what is worth reacting to and what is not. This is a learned sense that comes with experience – it's one of those things that cannot be taught. If you are a business veteran, then you probably have developed such a sense already. If not, and you are relatively new to the game, you would do well to seek out mentors to help you.

"From one thing, know ten thousand things." – Miyamoto Musashi

---

Chapter 20: Staying the Course

The nature of internet commerce is always in a degree of flux. Search algorithms, web technology, and social trends can change suddenly and drastically. The smartphone revolution changed the entire dynamic of online culture and commerce almost overnight. Business objectives and competitive environments shift and ebb every year. The speed and extent to which the internet changes means that businesses must operate against a backdrop of impermanence. What works today is not guaranteed to work tomorrow or next year.

The perpetual mutability of internet commerce can also foster huge opportunities for businesses – especially small ones. Social trends and technologies can emerge and propagate rapidly online. In many cases, these trends bring with them opportunities for businesses to expand their brands or sales. Small companies are particularly poised to exploit these opportunities compared to larger entities. Larger companies tend to have a longer chain of command for making decisions.

One mark of a canny online business leader or marketer is being able to detect and act upon opportunities when you see them. It starts with staying abreast of the current state of the internet, from cultural trends to technology. You should already be monitoring for social comments about your business and security threats, so add these to what you watch for. Look to identify opportunities within these trends to create sales, leads, or brand awareness. When you find them, take a step back to determine if the opportunity is real, appropriate, and one that is within your capacity to exploit. Act quickly, but do not jump in blindly – remember the cautionary tale about the #aurora hashtag from Chapter 16.

Never Stop Improving

At the beginning of this book, I likened a website to a garden – this analogy can now be applied to the entirety of your online business presence. No one part of your operation is ever finished or complete. Everything changes, and without regular supervision and maintenance, it will degrade just as a flower bed does. As flowers need regular trimming to generate new buds, so does your content. Flowers wilt with time just as social media posts become "stale" – necessitating a steady flow of new content. Unattended, even your finest paid ad campaigns will begin to underperform as competition responds. This is not unlike weeds creeping into a flowerbed.

It is important to maintain your online strategy with an eye toward continual improvement and growth. Do not settle for maintaining the status quo no matter how comfortable it might seem. Downturns in business can happen rapidly due to economic, social, or competitive factors. This can happen even more rapidly in the age of the internet. Having a growth-oriented marketing strategy creates a steady forward momentum against such inevitabilities. Maintaining the status quo is a form of stagnation and doing so puts your entire business at risk. Growth and improvement are the only inoculations against this.

Survival of the Fittest

Keep doing what works and stop doing what does not. Many marketers fall into emotional traps regarding their efforts. For instance, you might have an idea for a promotion that you are very proud of. This pride creates an emotional investment in its success. Should your idea end up being ineffective, your emotional connection to it might compel you to stick with it. After all, you reason, the idea is sound and success must be just around the corner. Admitting that a cherished idea is wrong is the mark of not just a good marketer, but also a mature person.

At every aspect and stage of your online operation, you should be evaluating efficacy. We covered various aspects of this in Chapters 8, 10, 18, and 19. Everything that you do online should have a purpose – it must exist in service of a specific objective. If it does not have a clear goal, then it should not exist, period. This paradigm applies to every webpage, social post, social share, PPC ad, influencer promotion, email, or blog post you create. In fact, the first step of everything you create online should be an affirmation of its goal. No goal equals no go.

Apply the concept of natural selection to your online content, posts, and advertising. If something works, as per measurable results, keep doing it and recreate it in future content. Ads that perform well should inform how you construct future ads. Popular blog posts will determine the subject of further blog content. Successful email newsletters indicate what your subsequent newsletters should be like. Conversely, poor-performing content should be selected for extinction. Delete your low performing ads. Unpopular blog or social posts should never be replicated or revisited. Everything you create online should be evaluated against their KPIs and judged accordingly. The unfit perish and the fit survive and propagate.

Staying Future-Proof

Staying informed on current on the state of the internet is part of the job for business leaders and marketers. You must be aware of what is going on both culturally and technologically. Nobody can authoritatively predict what comes next for the internet, but there are some presently clear trends (of this writing) that provide clues. There are numerous resources available that monitor and report on the state and trajectory of the internet, and they should be on your list of daily reading. A list of suggested resources can be found in the appendix.

Privacy

Easily one of the hottest topics about the future of the internet is privacy. The internet grew faster than the public or governments realized how much personal data internet companies came to control. Initially, this data only tracked time people spent sitting at their computers. The explosion of smartphones onto the scene changed things forever. Today, virtually everybody is connected online in some form 24/7. It is incontrovertible that the many conveniences of the internet could not have happened without service providers utilizing personal data. However, the extent to which this data was collected and catalogued turned out to be far broader and invasive than many imagined.

The 2010s saw the beginning of a major course-correction regarding internet data, and things show no signs of slowing down. Big changes have already happened. Internet companies like Google, Apple, Facebook/Meta, and Microsoft have become more transparent about data collection. Most have enabled users to control how their data is collected and used in a purely opt-in opt-out fashion. For many people and regulators, this is still not enough, and we can expect further changes in the future.

Regulation is coming. GDPR changed the landscape of internet privacy forever. It was the first of a new wave of online privacy regulations of such a large scale and scope. Regulators around the world are looking to GDPR as the starting point for how they craft their own native legislation.

Social Responsibilities

The recent rise of violent political extremism around the world has been directly linked to social media platforms. In the name of profitability, their algorithms fed extremist content to many of the most susceptible and volatile members of society. The insurrection of January 6th, 2021, at the US Capital was largely enabled by social media. In addition, the proliferation of conspiracy and anti-science misinformation online contributed to the spread of the COVID-19 pandemic. It is not an understatement that social media has proven to be a direct threat to the future of society and democracy itself.

The ramifications of extremism on social media have grabbed the attention of regulators and activists. Even social media companies are beginning to come around. Regardless, scrutiny on social media will continue to escalate so long as these threats remain. Regulatory actions are inevitable and voluntary changes have already happened. In early 2022, Meta announced that they would be disabling ad targeting for sensitive topics including health, science, religion, sexual orientation, and political movements. Other platforms have taken measures to reduce and penalize the spread of hate speech and extremist content. Time will tell how effective these initiatives will be, but they are likely only the beginning of a protracted war against online extremism.

AI and Machine Learning

More and more of the internet is being controlled by artificial intelligence, and this trend will continue. Complimentary to AI is machine learning, which is the capacity for AI to extrapolate data. What does this mean for internet commerce? We can expect to see AI taking over increasingly extensive parts of SEO and PPC campaigns. Google and Amazon already have optional AI-managed ad campaigns. Do not be surprised to see AI campaigns becoming mandatory in the future. Unfortunately, these AI will probably work harder to maximize revenue for their respective ad platforms than your bottom-line.

Search engines have always been based around machine learning, and they are only getting smarter. The ultimate goal for search is for it to be able to identify and index relevant content regardless of where it comes from or what format it is in. The holy grail in this space is where SEO is not necessary, because only the content matters. A perfect search engine should not need to have pages "optimized" for it to be seen. Time will tell if search ever reaches this point. For now, I will say that SEO professionals have job security...for now.

Demographic Shifts

Baby Boomers and Gen X are the last generations to remember a time before the internet. These groups have far more wealth than their younger peers, and so will continue to be core customers for many types of businesses even as their numbers shrink. They will also be the first large-scale audience who will require age-related accommodation from websites.

Millennials and Generation Z have had the internet for most or all their entire lives. Their culture was formed around the internet, and so their comfort level with technology is higher than any previous generation. To grow up with the internet was to grow up with rapidly changing technology, and so these groups will likely drive technological innovations their entire lives. They are comfortable with change. These groups, especially Gen Z, are highly diverse and more accepting and passionate for issues that involve equality and social justice. Consequently, they are very cognizant of the brands and businesses they support. Online businesses will be more scrutinized more and more for their roles in social issues like diversity, environmentalism, racism, personal freedom, LGBTQ+, democracy and more.

Customer Expectations

The internet has become an indispensable cornerstone of our lives and society. Not long ago, smart homes were for hobbyists and now they are common. The Alexa voice assistant is in millions of homes and video doorbells are commonplace. Broadband is everywhere and 5G wireless is expanding rapidly. The internet and connected handheld devices are the norm and no longer a novelty. People have high expectations from online businesses and services, and do not forget when they are not met.

Mobile devices are the dominant way in which people use the internet, and they will continue to demand full parity between mobile and desktop functionality. Any website entering development today and the future must be designed around mobile first. Where once mobile views were scaled down from the desktop, it is now the desktop view that scales from mobile.

Personalization

Personalization will continue to become the norm online, even in the face of privacy concerns. Websites will be designed around displaying dynamic content based on the user. This will extend to the nature of online pricing, which will programmatically target customer preferences and priorities. The same will hold true for discounts and offers. Furthermore, AI chatbots are continually improving and will soon be able to act as personal guides through websites.

Accessibility

Soon, website accessibility will *finally* become a top concern, especially as Boomers and Gen X continue to age. Since the beginning of the mainstream internet, disabled access has sadly not gotten the attention it deserves. In the US, the applicability of the Americans with Disabilities Act (ADA) to websites is murky at best. As a result, accommodation for disabled users is poor – despite them being a significant population with money to spend. Fortunately, the needs of an increasingly elderly population will force these long-overdue changes. Regardless, do the right thing now and get your website optimized for disabled users.

The Time We Have

I still remember the first moment I viewed the first website I ever worked on, back in 2003. I had finished installing and deploying the site backend, and so all I was looking at was a bare scaffolding of raw HTML and PHP. It was at that point where I wondered if I was making a career mistake - this was when the sting of the dotcom burst still reverberated. People did not trust the internet, and the idea of putting your credit card on the internet to buy things was scary. Some were even declaring the whole thing to have been nothing more than a fad.

So much has changed in the nearly twenty years since that day. Early on, you could rank a website on Google with keyword tricks and other chicanery. You didn't have to worry about your site accommodating mobile phones. Internet Explorer was the most popular browser. MySpace was the dominant social media platform. Connecting your website to other platforms was a chore, and enterprise software was quite primitive by todays' standards.

What I learned over twenty years is that the internet will always be in flux. Nothing is permanent, and lessons you learn today are not guaranteed to apply to tomorrow. In a way, the internet is an accelerated reflection of life and its impermanence. And therein lies the guiding principle I use when approaching online marketing strategies: everything changes, so keep moving, and never stop improving.

"Hard times are when a man has worked at a job for thirty years ... and they give him a watch, kick him in the butt and say 'hey a computer took your place, daddy'" – Dusty Rhodes

---

ABOUT THE AUTHOR

Gregory Shefler has worked in e-commerce for twenty years – starting out just as the dot com crash ended. During that time, he has played nearly every role there is in e-commerce: web developer; web designer; web administrator; graphic designer; copywriter; blogger; content manager; SEO; PPC, search, social, and Amazon marketer; analyst; privacy manager; price modeling; project manager; and many more.

His experience in such a multitude of roles informed his synergistic perspective of e-commerce and online marketing. He is a former senior leader and co-founder at Coffee Bean Direct, an online-based coffee company. Gregory currently provides consulting services for small online businesses. He is also an author having written this and his previous book, Noble Echoes - an exploration of the ethical dimension of the martial arts. Gregory can be reached at his website: gregoryshefler.com.

Made in the USA
Middletown, DE
09 February 2022

60863379R00176